'Families don't come in one size – nor does family r
Adcock lifts the lid on the theological underpinning ᴀ
with families of all shapes, stages and sizes. She lays
invites churches to explore theology and practice befo
Whether your church is just starting this journey or hᴀ_ ___.. _.. .. .ᴏ. ᴊ_.. .ᴇ ᴛ.ᴍᴇ, ᴛʜᴇʀᴇ ɪꜱ
plenty here to refresh your vision, understanding, strategy and practice.'
Mary Hawes, National Children and Youth Adviser, Church of England

'Gail Adcock's work is timely in a country facing uncertainty and turbulence, when we need
to nurture unity. Scratch the surface, and we find that creating and building family remains
of utmost importance to most people across all ages. The author's emphasis on adopting
a family-style intergenerational approach as a priority is prophetic and life-giving, not only
for the flourishing of church community, but for the health of society as a whole.'
**Caroline Dollard, Marriage and Family Life Adviser, Catholic Bishops' Conference of
England and Wales**

'Whether you're starting out working with families or you've been working in the field for
a while, this well-researched book of cultural and theological reflection combined with
practical wisdom will help you develop impactful ministry with families.'
Victoria Beech, creator of GodVenture

'Family ministry can be such a nebulous concept for churches to grapple with. What are
its boundaries? Is there even anything left for the rest of the church leadership to focus on
once we've listed everything we think the family ministry worker should be doing? In this
clear and concise book, Gail Adcock helps churches think theologically and strategically to
define family ministry for their setting. A must read for all church leaders as well as their
family ministry teams.'
**Sue Price, Hand in Hand Children's and Family Ministry Conference Director,
Kingsway CLC Trust**

'Gail's extensive knowledge and experience offers strong foundational principles and
examples of good working practice to resource family ministry. Covering aspects such as
the changes within family life and its impact on church life and ministry is helpful to set a
base from which the reader would be able to apply the material in a way that is relevant to
their context. Whether a leader or church is just starting out or has years of experience, this
book will be a valuable addition for use now and to be revisited as it offers such a wealth of
material that can be referred back to, enabling family ministry to be reviewed and adapted
to ensure it remains effective and relevant whatever the setting.'
Jane Butcher, Children and Families Pioneer, The Bible Reading Fellowship

The Bible Reading Fellowship
15 The Chambers, Vineyard
Abingdon OX14 3FE
brf.org.uk

The Bible Reading Fellowship (BRF) is a Registered Charity (233280)

ISBN 978 0 85746 578 8
First published 2020
10 9 8 7 6 5 4 3 2 1 0
All rights reserved

Acknowledgements
Unless otherwise stated, scripture quotations are taken from Holy Bible, New Living Translation, copyright © 1996, 2004, 2015 by Tyndale House Foundation. Used by permission of Tyndale House Publishers, Inc., Carol Stream, Illinois 60188. All rights reserved.

Scripture quotations marked NASB are taken from the New American Standard Bible®, Copyright © 1960,1962,1963,1968,1971,1972,1973,1975,1977,1995 by The Lockman Foundation. Used by permission.

Scripture quotation marked NIV is taken from the Holy Bible, New International Version (Anglicised edition) copyright © 1979, 1984, 2011 by Biblica. Used by permission of Hodder & Stoughton Publishers, a Hachette UK company. All rights reserved. 'NIV' is a registered trademark of Biblica. UK trademark number 1448790.

Every effort has been made to trace and contact copyright owners for material used in this resource. We apologise for any inadvertent omissions or errors, and would ask those concerned to contact us so that full acknowledgement can be made in the future.

A catalogue record for this book is available from the British Library

Printed and bound by TJ International.

THE ESSENTIAL GUIDE
TO FAMILY
MINISTRY

GAIL ADCOCK

To Matt, Luke and James.

I love and admire you all beyond measure.

Being family with you is a pure joy!

CONTENTS

ACKNOWLEDGEMENTS

The road to writing this book has been a long one, and there have been many people and places along the way that have influenced and shaped my thinking, theology and practice of family ministry. From those early days, when my own children were small and I began wondering what faith might look like for us at home, to the present, working and learning alongside fellow practitioners, it's been a fruitful journey of discovery at every turn.

To the church family of Winchester Road Methodist Church, who first introduced me to faith, thank you for being an all-age worshipping community who offered those early opportunities to belong and explore my gifts and abilities. Being church with you has hugely influenced my understanding of family beyond the four walls of home.

To those I've known at Stopsley Baptist Church, I'm grateful for your support, encouragement and risk-taking as we explored new opportunities and ways to be church with one another. In particular Pip Fleming, Jo Bird, David Painting, Ruth Deacon, Debbie Allen, Lysle Osbourne – each of you inspired me. Thank you for your partnership and generous spirit in using your gifts to see SBC's family work flourish and having the courage to try new things along the way.

To my Methodist colleagues, it continues to be a genuine pleasure to work alongside you and I'm grateful for the challenge, co-operation, laughter and determined hard work we do with each other. I have never known such a dedicated bunch of people so attuned to investing in making the church a better place for children, young people and families. You have evolved my thinking and practice in so many valuable ways. Special thanks to the CYF team for being such a fabulous bunch: Penny, Meg, Lynne, George and Jude.

Thank you to the team at BRF who have been great supporters of this book: Olivia, Dan, Jane and Rachel, I'm grateful for your patience and willingness to spur me on when the going got tough!

There are good friends from whom I've learnt much over the years and who encouraged me throughout the writing process: Penny C, Jo B, Amanda, Jo M, Jenny, Clare, Anne, Jo Y and Claire. Our families are all so diverse and you're each remarkable in how you face the challenges life brings. It's given me strength to have such resilient, brave, witty, generous and kind women in my life.

And finally, those special people I get to call my family. Thank you Mum and Dad for your love, eternal support and helping me believe I could achieve anything! My brother, Phil, even though you're no longer with us – you will always be a very precious part of my family and who I am; I think you'd be proud to see this. To the other three members of the Adcock Gang: Matt, Luke and James, what a privilege and delight it continues to be to grow as a family. The parenting learning curve has been immense, but, Luke and James, you've become fine men: keep walking your own path. Matt, I'm still enjoying the adventure of married life with you (never a dull moment); thank you for your kindness, love and unerring belief in me as I've been writing this. You are magnificent.

Thus far I have drawn a great deal of strength from the verses at the end of Isaiah 40, which talk of the everlasting God, that as we put our trust in him we do not grow weary or faint but instead will soar on wings like eagles. This is the God I continue to place my hope in every day.

FOREWORD

When I heard that Gail Adcock was writing *The Essential Guide to Family Ministry*, my first reaction was not just one of excitement, but also of relief. Family ministry has been a growing movement throughout the UK for many years, and we have a small set of key practitioners who have been pioneering the way forward for us throughout that time.

Most people, however, are like me. When I started in family ministry, I knew that it was important, but it also felt like being set adrift in a little boat on a vast ocean: the opportunities looked endless and there was very little to help me decide how to begin or what direction to head in. So I just began rowing, making up 'family ministry' as I went, making mistakes and learning from others as I tried to make progress but never really being sure that I was on the right or best route.

And that is why I am so grateful to Gail for writing this book. Family ministry is a crucial part of church, and it deserves practitioners who are not only passionate about doing it but also thoughtful and strategic about leading it. And *The Essential Guide to Family Ministry* helps us become those things.

Gail is one of the frontrunners of family ministry within the UK. She spent years of focused research across the country to find out what is already happening, how people think and engage with family ministry, and what the triumphs and struggles are of those in ministry. Her research was published in the *We Are Family* report and has formed the foundation of many deeper conversations about the ways forward for family ministry within the UK.

In this book, Gail combines her research with other international research and thinking and invites us into a journey of learning and innovation enabling us to become confident and strategic family ministers and leaders, not just people who do family ministry. Throughout the book, she partners solid theological exploration with practical, down-to-earth application, giving the reader solid ground on which to build their ministry. As I read my copy, I found myself highlighting the pages, jotting down notes and reflecting on my own church and ministry context, while also grabbing my Bible to reread a story or two that Gail gave me a different perspective on. She manages to take her vast reading of international research, theology and family-ministry practice and to package it up for me in such a light, easy, thought-provoking manner, so that I can instantly put into practice and conversation what I am learning as I read.

I am particularly excited about how Gail speaks from her own significant experience as a lay minister in her local church as well as her work at the national level. This book applies wisdom from the UK and other places to the areas and culture that we all operate within. She takes us on a journey of understanding the recent history and foundational theology of the family and helps us step back to see how the church, family and ministry can weave together to the benefit of all, right where we are.

I have learned so much from this book. I firmly believe that everyone who works within a church should read it, as this is not just about how children's, family and youth leaders can help parents more. *The Essential Guide to Family Ministry* challenges and equips how we all think about church, and what could happen when we invest in family ministry with purpose and passion.

Rachel Turner
Parenting for Faith Pioneer, The Bible Reading Fellowship

INTRODUCTION

Who is your ideal television or movie family? The one that stands out for you as being the epitome of family life? The one you'd just love to be part of – to share breakfast with or go on a camping trip with or simply hang out in the garden with, cooking on the barbecue while catching up on all that's happened in each other's lives in recent days?

Would you choose the celebrated animated family *The Simpsons* – Homer, Marge, Bart, Lisa and Maggie – who always seem to find themselves bounding from one calamity to the next? It might be appealing to be part of their chaotic home life – joining in with Homer's hapless escapades or Bart's mischief, while offering a sympathetic shoulder to the long-suffering Marge as she strives to maintain order.

Or maybe it would be *The Waltons* – the iconic extended family of John and Olivia, who with their seven children and John's parents live together in Depression-era rural Virginia? Their close-knit household endure trials of many kinds – illness, financial hardship and World War II. This is a family who cares for and supports each other and who struggle but who always make it through every up and down they face.

Or would you rather embrace the aristocracy and wealth of the Crawleys in *Downton Abbey*, living in majestic and opulent surroundings with the Earl of Grantham, his wife Cora, their daughters and loyal staff below stairs, including Carson, Bates and Mrs Patmore? Their privileged life has included a host of dramatic episodes – sometimes scandalous, often shocking and frequently romantic. It's never a smooth ride for anyone at Downton Abbey.

Perhaps you prefer a more contemporary extended family, such as the Pritchetts from *Modern Family*, and you enjoy the comic, larger-than-life characters and the experiences they have, which many of us can relate to.

Or perhaps a reality TV family is more your thing, and you'd love to be a part of the glitzy world that the Kardashians inhabit, soaking up the Hollywood lifestyle and revelling in the media frenzy that surrounds their day-to-day lives. The blurring of where reality ends and fiction begins could all be part of the appeal.

If these television families are recognisable, you probably have a range of responses to them, depending on your own family circumstances and past experience. Your instant reaction might be love or loathing – an affection for the characters or an intense dislike of them. Many of us will have those shows we've watched and longed to be a part of, even if simply to spend a day in that life; there's something about them we would like to experience or, even for just a short time, feel we belonged to. Sometimes TV families can create such incredible alternative worlds that, even if they're flawed and dysfunctional, the appeal of being part of their universe is strong. We can identify with their trials and triumphs, empathising with the roller-coaster ride of events and emotions this brings.

Fictional families (or those presented to us via a range of media per-spectives) inevitably lead us to make comparisons with our own families, becoming the ideal that we aspire to or indeed the exact opposite – that which we vow never to emulate. These television families are often upheld as representative of how the family exists in society today, and there is no doubt that there are elements of truth in the way they are depicted and that their roots lie in the real-life experiences of their writers and creators (Matt Groening, for example, acknowledges that the origins of the Simpsons lie in his own family). But whether they accurately reflect what it is to be a family today is definitely up for debate. They may reflect aspects of it, but they can never truly epitomise the authentic day-to-day lived experience of being family.

For churches, organisations and individuals working with or supporting families, this reality can be bewildering. Where do we even start? As the church has begun to reflect more seriously on how it can be a force for good in the home, it's still playing catch-up with how families have changed. Grappling with both theology and practice, we're striving to acclimatise so that our approaches are relevant to those we seek to serve. It can seem as if we have a mountain to climb. Our established models for family ministry often no longer reflect the communities and people they seek to serve. Over time a chasm has opened up between families and the church, where neither one recognises the other or believes it is possible to establish a mutually fulfilling rapport. We need to examine afresh the strategy, structure and purpose of our family ministry.

Television exerts a powerful influence; it holds a mirror up to society and reflects what is valued. Yet what it doesn't show, as the family ministry writer and researcher Diana Garland argues, is equally as important: 'What television did not portray also provides an interesting perspective on how our culture saw itself.'[1] Television can never fully convey the diverse and complex nature of family life experienced by people day to day in households across the UK.

The portrayal of family life on screen does offer us an indication of how far the social context occupied by families has changed in the past 100 years. From the clearly defined class backdrop of *Downton Abbey* in the early 20th century, where all know their place, to the wealthy, media-savvy influence of the Kardashians, and all that lies in between, what it means to be a family has become much more flexible. Even in the last half-century, contemporary family life has evolved so that today we see a complex new environment that would be barely recognisable to families of the post-war era. From family roles, employment opportunities and domestic arrangements to leisure time and the type of meals we put on the table (or on the tray in front of the television), there is little of everyday family life that resembles those of the generations before us.

However, across the church there remains a strong desire to meet families where they are. In the midst of families forging new ways of being in the 21st century, people in lay ministry, church leaders and volunteers are all committed to providing the care and support families need in order to thrive. Churches in cities, towns and villages are seeking to be places that offer a welcome and generous hospitality to parents and children in their communities, and the sheer breadth of ways they do this is highly commendable; from toddler groups, through lunch clubs to all-age church services, there's a multitude of activities that fall under the banner of family ministry. Against a backdrop of families evolving into new forms, creating their lives together in new ways, there's an indisputable need for the church to be more fully informed if these ministries and provisions are going to have an effective impact.

The aim of this book is to be a guide through this unfamiliar territory. It begins with an exploration of the theory and setting for ministry to families today, grounded in a rich theology that calls us to be inspired by divine ideas and precedents. This first part of the book provides us with an opportunity to embed what we believe as Christians in the contemporary family landscape and ensures we have a firm foundation upon which to grow and develop our ministry. The guide then moves on, in the next part, to the principles underpinning all aspects of exceptional ministry to families, combining these with an understanding of our practice. Viewed together through the lens of our own contexts, these have the potential to become seven habits for highly effective family ministry (to adapt the title of Stephen Covey's bestseller[2]) enabling us to establish practices in our everyday work that are truly transformative and beneficial for all.

Whatever families we find ourselves supporting and nurturing, wherever we find ourselves ministering to them, let's invite God to lead and equip us for all that's in store. May these words from Psalm 90 bless and encourage you as we embark on an adventure together in the coming pages, in the knowledge that God is with us:

Satisfy us each morning with your unfailing love,
so we may sing for joy to the end of our lives.
Give us gladness in proportion to our former misery!
Replace the evil years with good.
Let us, your servants, see you work again;
let our children see your glory.
And may the Lord our God show us his approval
and make our efforts successful.
Yes, make our efforts successful!
PSALM 90:14–17

I

MINISTRY AND FAMILIES TODAY

1

THE CHANGING SHAPE OF FAMILY

Introduction

In the mid 1920s, my nan grew up with her siblings in a house in London that was just a few doors down from her grandparents. On the same street lived aunts, uncles and cousins, so every day contained some form of contact with her wider family. Whether it was popping in to say hello after school, getting a bite to eat or playing together, family were always on hand. After she was married, Nan and my granddad made their home on the same road and until the last few years of her life remained in that house. For Nan, family life was very much rooted in that place, and she enjoyed close relationships with family members nearby.

Skip to the present day and this type of lived family experience is becoming rarer and rarer, essentially becoming confined to the past. As children enter adulthood today, they rarely stay in the same area as where they were raised. Work and education can require a move away, and new relationships often mean a new location. Extended families now find themselves scattered the length and breadth of the country, separated by hundreds of miles or, if they've taken the bold decision to build a new life in another country, thousands. Grandparents, parents, children and relatives may not live in the same village, town or city, so how they seek to be family with and for each other bears little resemblance to the more informal daily contact enjoyed a century previously. Of course, that's not to say that families today don't experience closeness or the same depth of family ties;

it's simply that the way this is created or lived out looks very different. All this reflects the way our understanding of what family is, how it's formed and how it functions has evolved and developed over time.

Events of the 20th century provide the backdrop to this evolution. Rapid changes in industry, technology, education, politics, gender roles, and societal groups and attitudes have all transformed the way we live and interact. With two world wars enormously impacting both society as a whole and individual families, it comes as no surprise that the rate of change has had consequences that are still reverberating through people's lives today. The changes taking place in homes and relationships at a domestic level interact with wider cultural, economic and demographic shifts. It's perhaps no wonder that we face so many questions about what it means to be family in the 21st century. If we want to be able to authentically meet the needs of families we know and support, it's vital that we grasp how these changes have shaped them. This chapter seeks to explore some of the significant developments that have taken place in the UK and the way they have filtered through to affect the everyday lives of parents, children, carers and members of their extended families.

Diverse family forms

Throughout the 19th and 20th centuries, there has been a prevailing narrative in western culture: that the family is in decline.[3] As changes in family structure become visible and new forms of family evolve, the cry of the traditional family being in disarray, and that this is causing the breakdown of social cohesion and ultimately the collapse of community, is unmistakable. This view is often held by traditionalists and politicians who seek to adopt and implement policies that will halt further change, reinforcing traditional family models.

We tend to think of this narrative as decrying the decline of the nuclear family, but in reality the nuclear family is a more recent development. Up until the beginning of the 20th century, families were extended, multigenerational units that functioned together – providing mutual care, earning a living, sharing space and often living under the same roof, doing life in a way that met the needs of all members and ensured its ability to provide for young and old alike. This practical approach to family transitioned in the early decades of the 20th century to smaller groupings, which became the norm: 'The new, lean, nuclear family of the 1950s comprised two parents and two children who lived independently from grandparents or other relatives.'[4] As a result of economic and social factors, families began to function in reduced, more concise forms, altering in membership and relationship. (Diana Garland argues, however, that the nuclear family has its roots much earlier in history – that these traditional forms of family existed in the Middle Ages.[5]) The nuclear family captures in essence the notion of family being a consanguineous group – that is, related to one another by blood ties – and having a shared bond of commitment. It is a model based on the marriage of a man and woman, who each adopt specific roles and make particular contributions to household life, raising children together (often limited to two or three, hence the stereotype of families with 2.4 children).

Considering its relatively recent appearance, the nuclear family has become a solid institution culturally, impacting on political policy and bringing with it the notion of 'family values', now widely held. The nuclear family is perceived to offer the ideal context for raising children, providing stability and an environment that encourages them to flourish. Academic research, including the influential study *Family and Kinship in East London* by Michael Young and Peter Willmott in the 1950s, 'showed how far the nuclear family, as a social institution, had adapted to meet the demands of modern society'.[6] It had in a short space of time become the model that all family forms and functions were held up against, compared to and contrasted with, occupying a position that declared it to be the ideal. Yet Garland believes this has been detrimental to our broader understandings of family: 'Our cultural embrace of the nuclear family as the ideal has blinded us to the importance of kinship based on family commitments other than those formed by legal marriage and biology.'[7] By elevating the status of the nuclear family, the value and contribution made by other forms has been overlooked and dismissed. The diversity of how family is created and experienced can be lost in the pursuit of a narrow definition that doesn't allow for broader forms to be explored or included.

More recently the breadth of contemporary family structures that exist has been increasingly apparent, and the focus of research has shifted from purely a study of the formation of family to more nuanced investigations of how it is practised. Interest has arisen in how family members relate to each other as family, moving away from fixed definitions to more fluid understandings, as Fiona Williams explains: 'It registers the ways in which our networks of affection are not simply given by virtue of blood or marriage but are negotiated and shaped by us, over time and place.'[8]

This was highlighted by the Family Ministry Research Project, in its report *We Are Family*, which explored who family workers met, supported and ministered to in the course of their church roles, indicating the variety of groupings that are collectively described as 'family'.[9] Twelve types of family were identified, capturing a diverse range of family structures and forms that exist in the UK today. These included married or cohabiting couples with or without children or adult offspring; blended families; lone parents raising children; families from a range of ethnic and faith groups; same-sex couples with children; fostered and adopted children in families; extended families; children with additional needs in families; and family members who had assumed carer responsibilities for another. The variety of forms indicates that many churches are actively seeking to offer ministry and support to all types of family, regardless of structure. It reflects a significant move towards embracing family diversity, moving away from traditional perceptions of the church solely extending support and ministry to the nuclear family. Family ministry practitioners adopt broad definitions of what constitutes family and frequently strive to make their programmes and activities accessible to all. The omission of single people from the research project did not go unnoticed but may suggest they continue to be considered outside the scope of family work.

Of course, the types of family mentioned above are not recent additions to the social and cultural landscape – they have always existed yet rarely been recognised. Only recently have these more diverse forms become more visible. Williams acknowledges this, saying that this short-sightedness was because such forms 'did not fit the normative picture of family life'.[10] She believes it's crucial to make a distinction between 'normative family' (how it 'ought' to be) and the 'lived experiences' (how it is worked out in practice) of family lives as these ideas impact upon one other. Her phrase 'the contours of family lives'[11] helpfully illustrates the notion of developing everyday family life and experience that many practitioners will be only too aware of.

Since the 1990s new approaches to understanding the family have been evolving. Studies have adopted the concept of 'family practices', wanting to explore how members 'do family life' together. David Morgan has been a central proponent of this approach and highlighted 'the need to define families by their customs and practices rather than exclusively by co-residence or even simply by kinship and marriage'.[12] This emphasis on 'doing' over structure, seeking to better understand how a sense of family is created rather than who individual family members are, provides an enormously helpful insight into the complexities of being family today. It provides a sharper lens through which to view the challenges and joys that are faced by a diverse range of families, which in turn can inform the ministry and support that churches choose to make available.

Adopting a 'family functioning' framework for viewing families makes possible the recognition of a variety of relationships and that for many the bonds of friendship have grown to become similar to those experienced by blood relatives. If family is identified through 'invoking the quality of a relationship marked by closeness, confiding, sharing and mutuality',[13] then many people would classify friendships as family, something that is becoming more common in households. Although family structure and shape as observed today can be very fluid and continues to develop, the sense of commitment that members have to each other has not altered. For families there is often a motivation to 'do the right thing', remaining connected and committed to one another, as indicated in the research programme on Care, Values and the Future of Welfare (CAVA).[14] This may be commitment expressed differently, but still 'little of this indicates a loss of commitment itself, but rather suggests that the mesh of those commitments which contain people's close, caring and intimate relationships is patterned differently'.[15] Families continue to understand the depth of obligation required to other members and remain devoted to one another, whether they share blood ties or simply have chosen to be family for and with one another.

Although traditional forms of family may no longer be the primary model observed in society, the diverse forms we encounter today often subscribe to many of the same values which are fundamental in our relationships with other human beings. For those working and ministering in this field, there is an urgency to create new frameworks through which contemporary families can be better understood and more effectively reached.

Shifting gender roles

Alongside these changes in family form and structure, recent decades have seen developments in the way that family members operate and engage with each other. The impact of these developments is being felt in myriad ways, not least in how families exist and function domestically, as well as more widely, in the spheres of work and education. Since the end of World War II, the traditional model of men going out to work and women remaining home has been in decline, and a more flexible framework for adult employment has emerged. More women are in paid employment, whether full- or part-time, than at any point in living memory – in 1971 52% of women were employed, rising to 72% in early 2019.[16] In contrast the percentage of men working has gradually fallen since the early 1970s, from 92% in 1971 to 80% in 2019.

While the decline in male employment could be due in part to a fall in manufacturing jobs, traditionally male roles, for women the statistics tell a different story – more are seeking out financial and personal independence through joining the employment market. This is partly a result of the ongoing changes in the state pension age for women. Women have also been central in filling roles across the service sector, especially within the care and leisure fields, where an increase in jobs has been evident. Changes in legislation have also made an impact on women's ability to access and retain greater opportunities across the working environment. It's also worth mentioning that men with children are more likely to work than those without, whereas the opposite picture for women is observed.

The nature of employment has also become more fluid, often no longer conforming to a standard nine-to-five pattern; increasingly part-time roles and shift work are the norm. Full-time paid employment no longer offers a route out of poverty. These circumstances provide challenges and dilemmas for many parents, concerning their ability not only to provide for their families financially but also to create and invest in their life together. For parents, the struggle to maintain work commitments while managing home life and childcare has become like trying to solve a complex jigsaw puzzle – constantly reconfiguring plans in a manner that leads to surviving rather than thriving. Many reflect that they rarely feel they achieve a healthy balance between the two.

Working Families is a UK organisation that helps working parents, carers and employers find a better balance between responsibilities at home and work. In its *Modern Families Index 2017* it reported high levels of dissatisfaction among parents. This reflected the fact that trying to combine work and home life was an increasing source of stress and was having a negative effect on family relationships and that families were finding it more and more difficult to spend time together. For some, particularly younger parents, this pressure has led to burnout. Finding working solutions and compromising where necessary are often a route parents struggle to navigate. As Working Families reports, 'Family remains the greatest priority for working parents but balancing the increasing pressures of work is taking its toll, with only a third of parents leaving work on time every day.'[17]

Gender equality at work (with related issues of childcare) has moved rapidly up the employment agenda in recent decades. While great progress has been made, many women continue to experience disparity and discrimination in the workplace, battling to gain the same rights as their male counterparts. As Jessica Woodroffe highlights, 'Motherhood has a direct and dramatic influence on women's pay and employment prospects, and typically this penalty lasts a lifetime.'[18]

The profile of shared parental leave has grown since the Children and Families Act 2014 was passed, extending the right for employees to request flexible working. Yet the reform it sought to bring is still a long way from becoming embedded in our usual employment practices and bringing about genuine culture change. Equal pay and access to senior positions, where women are often poorly represented, continue to be prominent campaigning issues.

Against this backdrop, there has been an inevitable impact on the lived experience of many families at home. How families function within their four walls has transformed from what it was just a few decades previously. The well-defined male and female domestic roles of the past have become increasingly blurred. Twentieth-century sociological thinking around family has grounded ideas of the nuclear family in notions of 'need' and 'function'. Adopting a narrow definition of family meant that other forms came to be seen as abnormal and undesirable. Talcott Parsons considered the nuclear family to be 'the most efficient unit for dealing with the challenges of modern society through a specialization of roles between husband and wife'.[19] He asserted this to be the primary mode of how family *should* be formed, locating the theory in a distinct framework defined by gender. However, these views came under substantial criticism and were ultimately discredited as further research was undertaken towards the end of the century. The shift in family roles towards more egalitarian approaches demonstrates a need to see beyond gender stereotypes. It offers an opportunity to reassess how parents and carers share domestic responsibilities, balancing work and home life between them.

Of course, notions of 'women's work' continue to exist. As Chambers stresses, 'The gendered division of labour within two-parent households remains surprisingly persistent, with research findings continuing to highlight deep-rooted gendered practices in the allocation of domestic and paid work.'[20] But there are signs that family relationships and responsibilities are slowly becoming more democratic. The task of parenting as a predominantly female activity is gradually being dismantled as traditional perceptions of roles are eroded. Many parents are now much more intentional about sharing the load of raising children. Yet flexible working practices and the cost of childcare brings new and often complex issues with no simple solutions.

For Williams, this indicates the era of transition we are in: 'The old exists in the new and the new in the old.'[21] That is, it is not clear-cut whether these changes in families are leading to the decline of the family or to a new equality. There are huge variations in the way these changes are working their way through family lives and how people balance parenting and work commitments.

Adapting family lifestyle

These changes to how families function in relation to each other, and the roles they hold both within and beyond the home, have impacted upon the day-to-day experience of being a family. The kind of lifestyle a family adopts can determine a wide range of factors around how they live with one another as a household. Significantly, changes in the world of work, particularly the higher number of women in the workforce, have caused life at home to change. While this move away from the male-breadwinner model of family in theory represents progress for women, in practice it has led to greater tension in work-life balance, particularly for women. This is because, as Janet Finch and Jennifer Mason indicate, 'Women are still the primary carers and "kinkeepers".[22] The shifts that have occurred in the working lives of women have not been matched by a change in the responsibilities and expectations of men in the domestic environment. Many women, therefore, find themselves trying to maintain traditional roles of housekeeper and mother alongside paid employment, and it is difficult to meet the expectations of both worlds of duty and experience a sense of satisfaction. Even in households where fathers are more actively engaged in the raising of their children, there is often still not an equal sharing of housework.

The predominance of women as the primary caregiver characterises many family relationships, particularly in the raising of children from infancy to adulthood. According to Williams, women provide care to others in myriad ways, including 'helping, tending, looking out for, thinking about, talking, sharing, and offering a shoulder to cry on'.[23] The vital role of women in contributing to a family's sense of well-being cannot be underestimated.

Another lifestyle change in recent decades has been the increase in leisure time, alongside the notion of parents spending 'quality time' with their children. How families choose to spend their weekends, the kinds of activities they participate in and the places they visit have become significant choices they make outside of working hours. Spending time together socially, relaxing, enjoying sport or creative activities are seen increasingly as an essential aspect of family life and less a treat or extravagance. In earlier decades 'free time' would have been a peculiar concept, with time outside of work spent tending to essential home maintenance or doing simple activities such as reading books or newspapers, listening to the radio, playing games or, for children, spending time outdoors, a practice much less common today. With the rise of the smartphone and tablet, much of a family's spare time is consumed online – shopping, interacting on social media or gaming. The impact this has on family relationships and on our ability to form strong bonds in the home is the source of much debate, yet there is evidence that technology has provided new opportunities for families to connect and enjoy each other's company. Regardless of our views in this arena, we recognise the notion of having 'digital' lives, and that our online presence isn't a disconnected virtual one but very much an extension of our physical existence. For parents to be aware, engaged and supportive of their children as they grow in the digital world is vital.

For many households, less time today is spent gathering with extended family. These types of family get-togethers were more regular and frequent a few decades ago, when they were a common part of family life alongside the rites of passage that mark our lives, such as weddings and funerals. That they are less common today is due often to geography – families can appear to be less connected with blood relatives if they have moved away for study, work or affordable housing. The networks that earlier generations were part of, often local and easily available, are no longer to be found. For many people, support needs to be found elsewhere, often with others who are at a similar life stage, as Williams indicates: 'Self-help groups play an important role in communities in providing the sort of care and support that people say they want: that is, based on reciprocity, trust, mutual respect, informality and being non-judgemental'[24] – all of which are qualities previously considered to be benefits of family ties. In today's globalised culture our web of commitments can extend further than any time in history, whether ties of blood, marriage or friendship. Support networks are being created in new, innovative ways that allow families, parents and children to flourish and remain connected in our continually digitally developing world.

The trend towards geographically dispersed extended family may be changing. The Office for National Statistics (ONS) reports that multi-generational households (those containing two or more families) 'were the fastest growing household type over the decade to 2015, increasing by 50% from 197,000 households in 2005 to 295,000 households in 2015'.[25] There could be a variety of reasons for this shift, which coincides with greater numbers of young adults opting to remain in the family home (with men more likely than women to do so). The ONS highlights that those living together may or may not be blood relatives but that 'changes in the number of multi-family households may be because of older couples moving in with their adult child and their family, young adults who are partnered or lone parents remaining in or returning to their parent's households and unrelated families sharing a household'.[26]

Young adults are becoming more aware of the advantages of remaining at home or being in closer proximity to their family. Beyond the socio-economic benefits, the notion of parental influence may be a key factor for this: 'The positive effect of one's parents' presence dissipates gradually with distance, not sharply at the border of a neighbourhood.'[27]

Since the 1980s, government policy influencing family life, particularly in relation to raising children, has shifted. As concerns around child protection and safeguarding have grown, so has the amount of legislation to ensure the priority of a child's well-being and security. As Williams says, 'Parenthood and parenting have become less a private matter',[28] so there has been a rise in regulations around parental responsibility.

In parallel, widespread debates around 'good parenting' have arisen, along with the development of schools of thought pushing a particular approach. Older styles or approaches to parenting are often discarded in favour of notions of 'quality time' or 'attachment', for instance. Parenting styles can be a polarising topic; when combined with increased anxiety about 'getting it wrong', it can leave many parents feeling confused or guilty and lacking confidence when striving to raise children. Parenting has become a very public activity, especially with the rise of social media. All now feel able to comment on and criticise, which can undermine a parent's ability to seek help and support in times of difficulty. In contrast the status of a couple's relationship is far less important. Whereas a few decades ago the possibility of separation or divorce would have been morally and socially unacceptable, in the 21st century much less attention is given to the marital status of couples. Cohabiting is common, with outdated notions of morality, such as 'living in sin', no longer a barrier to couples wanting to create a household of their own.

Conclusion

Our understanding of how family life is experienced in the 21st century is challenging earlier notions of what it means to be family and how and where family is created. Our perceptions are shifting and new theories are emerging. In this chapter we sought to explore the wealth of change in Britain in recent decades:

- *Diverse family forms* – although the family of 'married couple with children' still dominates, there is growing evidence of family being created in different environments for a range of factors, including economic, employment and schooling opportunities, and there is a wider array of family structures, with parents, partners, husbands, wives and children being family to and for each other in a host of different households.

- *Shifting gender roles* – men and women are still coming to terms with these changes, and society continues to wrestle with questions around their roles. In particular the care of children and elderly relatives is a much-debated topic; where the lines of responsibility lie and how provision is offered continue to challenge many.

- *Adapting family lifestyle* – the edges between work and home life are increasingly blurred. Finding networks for support can be challenging for families who live long distances from blood relatives, and establishing these in their local community can often prove fruitful. The 'digital revolution' has meant families often communicate differently, and parents need to be alert to the issues it raises.

With so much unprecedented change, it's perhaps not surprising that there is a new challenge facing us in churches when seeking to reach out missionally and pastorally to the families we encounter. Our long-held approaches to ministry are no longer effective or bearing fruit as they may have done for previous generations. The emphasis on the nuclear family as the ideal, a view held in many churches, puts it at odds with the lived experience of many in society. It's foolish to assume that any two families will be the same, possess the same values or have the same priorities. Each will make their own choices based on a range of factors from their own upbringing, culture, job and income, circumstances and pressures. Different generations will have their own parenting preferences – opting to raise their children in ways reflecting their own roots or choosing to embrace new methods based on individual experience and observation.

With such a broad and diverse landscape within which ministry now takes place, there is a simple lesson: know *your* families. There is nothing more important than having a distinct understanding of the types of families in our neighbourhoods: those who use the local supermarket, play at the local park, attend the local school and spend time down the local pub. This knowledge is vital. If our work, ministry and support is to be authentic, relevant and life-giving, this must be the place we start.

Understanding the impact these different factors have on families is another priority. Reconciling the demands of work with the responsibilities of parenting and home life is a huge dilemma for many families. There is much we could do to alleviate some of this pressure, or at least we can acknowledge the modern stresses that are difficult to balance. Exploring approaches that lessen the load could prove enormously beneficial to many families in connection to their local church.

Finally, what of faith? What of encountering God in the midst of so much rich, diverse and continually evolving life that has joys and struggles? In this transformed environment there are exciting new opportunities to meet God at work with parents, children and their extended families, and witness him love unconditionally, bring hope and bring new understanding of who he is. There is an extraordinary calling upon us to join God in the thick of what he does naturally – draw all things to himself so that we better experience the divine in our everyday lives as family.

Questions for reflection

Spend some time either individually or with your congregation or church leadership considering these questions. If you're unsure of the response, this could be a prompt to go and find out.

- Who are the kinds of families you meet where you live?

- What do you see of how parents juggle their work-life balance? Where do you observe the pressure points?

- How do the families you know like to spend their free time?

2

THEOLOGY FOR FAMILY MINISTRY

Introduction

With the vibrant diversity of contemporary family experience that we reflected on in the previous chapter, we might anticipate that there has been a lot of thinking on the theology of family. Yet even brief research on the topic reveals very much the contrary. There is a significant lack of theological reflection being done around our understandings of and belief about the family and its function and place in church and society. It appears to have been neglected, Adrian Thatcher says, along with related fields, such as children – left at the fringes of theology while other matters hog the limelight.[29] What theological thinking there has been is often generated from what Jack and Judith Balswick describe as 'bouquets of verses',[30] snippets of scripture that have been detached from their context and origin, only to be reassembled and repurposed to serve an alternative agenda.

This lack seems odd for two reasons. First, family is the foundation of much of our everyday life, impacting on all of us in some shape or form. It collides frequently with our perceptions of the nature of God, how we encounter and build relationship with him and what it means to belong to the community he calls us to, the church.

Second, the subject of family is potentially rich to explore theologically – to strive to relate our experiences to scripture, to untangle the understandings we've inherited down the generations and to try to make sense of how and where we meet with God in the array of difficult, exciting, challenging, hopeful, frustrating and joyous times that make up our life together as family.

So why aren't we more determined and united in our desire to see theological reflection grow in this field? We have much contemplation and learning to do.

Perhaps one of the barriers is something we've already alluded to. Rather than the wealth of contemporary family experience being something to inspire us to reflect on belief more deeply, it becomes a hindrance, overwhelming us. We're reluctant to explore theological understandings of family partly because family is so diverse today – it's not easily contained or summarised. It's virtually impossible to gather so many perspectives into a coherent train of thought when it may ignore or diminish some of those families and their members. If our hope is to develop an authentic family theology that is broadly reflective of what we see and hear of family life, then its roots need to be in the day-to-day experience of being a family. Separating our thinking from concrete experience would undermine it entirely. Finding ways to unite belief and practice is a challenge, but that shouldn't stop us trying. Even if it brings us to only a partially formed understanding, the process would surely have been fruitful.

Getting beyond the explicit and implicit beliefs we have about family can also be a stumbling block. Each of us will have our own understanding and assumptions about what family is, or should be, formed by our own experiences, both from our childhoods and as we've grown to have families of our own, and by the teaching we've received in faith settings and church services. These will in turn influence our theology. Traditional and historical views of what family is and of what scripture says family should be can often conflict with what we currently see or know from the families we encounter. Drawing together these different strands of thought and belief can hinder our pursuit of developing a clear and cohesive approach to practice, as each have distinct notions and ideas.

Our understanding of family and household in western society in the 21st century differs vastly from that of the early church in the Middle East. The very concept of family evolves through time and place, which in turn influences the basis of our theology. Diana Garland, in her comprehensive guide to family ministry, offers an informative summary of how historical understandings of family have developed in Christian thought and teaching.[31] With terms such as 'family values' regularly bounced around in the same space as ideas of 'family decline', it's easy to see how misunderstanding has arisen. Confusing our theology with the notion of values is often unhelpful; through developing family theology we might be able to establish more constructive approaches to ministry with families, approaches that aren't seeking to perpetuate family structures but rather give life to new modes of being which enhance family life and encourage families in their shared lives together.

One of the most significant recent ventures exploring belief around family has been the work directed by Don Browning of the University of Chicago's Religion, Culture, and Family Project. It has sought to address issues on family from a non-denominational perspective, grounding its principles in practical theology and advocating for 'egalitarian family'. As Thatcher states, this work 'wrestles with the key question "Is it the quality of family experience, rather than the form, that Christianity celebrates? Or is it both quality and form that it values?"'[32] The project has been hugely influential and played a vital role in seeking to unravel some of the fundamental questions that continue to challenge and provoke a wide spectrum of opinions about family today. There is an obvious danger in pursuing too narrow a doctrine of family, which results in many feeling excluded and beyond the welcome or hospitality of the church. Garland proposes an alternative approach, one of 'nets cast out to gather in all kinds rather than as sieves controlling what goes into the boat called the church'.[33]

When we take as our starting point an authentic understanding of contemporary family life, we have an opportunity to rediscover new and vibrant theological perspectives. In conjunction with readings of scripture, such a starting position could open the door to new understandings of God's intentions for us as we live in community with one another. This chapter seeks to visit some of the common theological beliefs around notions of family, including Trinitarian views, inviting us to reflect and develop our own understandings. It also seeks to offer a springboard into greater reflection, urging us to be engaged in an ongoing wrestling with our beliefs and practice of family life.

Let's explore, then, the question of 'what do we believe about family?' When we reflect on scripture, what might it be saying to us? What can we learn from it about God's engagement with and hope for families?

Three theological perspectives

1 Holiness at home

Images and mentions of family in scripture are numerous throughout both the Old and New Testaments. There's a wealth of narrative that offers a glimpse of God's purpose and hope for families. However, it would be easy to arrive at the conclusion, based on many of the families encountered in scripture, that there's little to hold up by way of example! As David and Diana Garland remind us, 'The family tree of the Messiah reveals a family whose closets seem to be bursting with skeletons.'[34] Jesus' ancestry presents a host of families struggling to relate, make good choices and seek the best for each other.

This shouldn't surprise us. Scripture contains very human stories that often reflect much of what we continue to experience and see around us today. We meet households and family members who time after time demonstrate that all is not well, treating each other with contempt, illustrating a raw and often ugly underside to their family relationships. Yet, as we read the tales of deception, violence and betrayal, we learn from these very real struggles and we catch glimpses of God's grace and mercy, revealing to us more of his nature and his hope for those he has created. Rather than presenting an unattainable ideal of family, scripture shares the harsh reality of the difficulties experienced by all families at different points.

Nevertheless God's calling is a high one, exhorting families to be environments that cultivate holiness. In Deuteronomy 6, a well-known passage relating to family ministry, we are given a compelling picture of a faithful household:

> Listen, O Israel! The Lord is our God, the Lord alone. And you must love the Lord your God with all your heart, all your soul, and all your strength. And you must commit yourselves wholeheartedly to these commands that I am giving you today. Repeat them again and again to your children. Talk about them when you are at home and when you are on the road, when you are going to bed and when you are getting up. Tie them to your hands and wear them on your forehead as reminders. Write them on the doorposts of your house and on your gates.
>
> DEUTERONOMY 6:4–9

Moses has just returned from a powerful encounter with God and brings the ten commandments before his people, giving a heartfelt and impassioned call to put God first, to follow him with their whole being, to let their whole lives be filled with and led by a desire to place him first. And yet it's not a message just for the adults – it's a family affair. Homes are to be places where these commandments become a way of life for people of all ages, woven into the very rituals of their day-to-day life.

Here we learn how, as parents, we have a primary responsibility to embed faith and God into our daily lives. It's a 24/7, round-the-clock way of being. Our children are to grow in the knowledge that faith goes beyond Sunday worship services; it is the bedrock of how we live, the choices we make and how we grow in love and understanding of who God is.

Within the broader story in Deuteronomy of God's people being called to worship the one and only true God, we as families learn how to place him at the heart of our lives together. This requires our entire being to be intentionally leaning in to who God is, embracing him and all he desires for us. Our discipleship is to be woven into the very fabric of our daily lives, through all those routine practices that form our lived experience with one another. These verses picture faith as firmly embedded in the day-by-day ups and downs of family life; it should and certainly not be contained purely in our Sunday activities in churches and services. It's a compelling reminder of the central place God has in humanly busy and demanding lives, and for him to remain there requires our ongoing commitment to being reminded of who he is and all he has accomplished.

Deuteronomy 6 is also a reminder of the essential role parents and carers have in nurturing faith at home: being a 'domestic church', a household that together seeks God, a community that has its own story of faith to share. Families shape an authentic faith ecosystem that features adults being 'in conversation with children about what they are experiencing as they encounter God'.[35] There's a subtle difference here, important to recognise, from the idea of 'passing on the faith', an oft-used phrase suggesting that adults retain the power to extend or withhold faith from children, frequently associated with this passage. Instead it's a picture of families embracing relationship with God equally, their discipleship growing alongside one another, mutually impacting and nurturing. The flow of faith isn't so much directed from parents and carers down to children; rather, it moves freely between them as they each experience God in their own distinct way.

There's an enormous difference between perceiving faith as a bolt-on, an aspect of life that has little connection to the rest of our lives, and it being like a carpet underlay that we walk upon constantly. What's being presented by Moses here in Deuteronomy is a call to cultivate holy households and faith in God for everyone, from the very youngest members of the community through to those in their later years. We encounter the notion here of being set apart and different, that as we grow in our understanding of being God's people and deepen our relationship with him, we're establishing holy households.

For us and our families, God is placed at the centre, closely followed by a desire to work out our high calling from Deuteronomy 6, to love him with all our heart, soul and might. The mutuality of our whole family loving and being loved in this way impacts on us profoundly as we live and breathe and do life together in our households. As we love God, so we love others. This forms a holy care in our homes. Garland places care at the centre for family faith: our care and love for each other in our family units are extended to others around us in a range of hospitable ways. This is the demonstration of the gospel as we widen the circles of care and influence around us. In this way, as Garland writes, 'The ordinary is sacred, and the sacred is ordinary.'[36] Our households become holy places where we abide in care: being cared for and caring for others.

I wonder how you react to that word 'holy'. Does it sit well with you or make you feel uncomfortable? Is it a word that has positive and helpful connotations for you? We might assume that holiness refers to living a pious life – rising early every morning to read the Bible, carving out hours each day to pray. Yet if we dig a little deeper, we discover holiness to be a much more multifaceted concept: it goes beyond our ideas of spiritual disciplines or 'other worldliness'. The booklet *Holiness and Justice*, created to support a recent presidential year in Methodism, outlines a number of central ideas that are helpful as we explore our understanding of faith at home. It includes, among others, these five ideas:[37]

- *Wonder and amazement* – Those times when we've experienced a sense of awe and wonder, perhaps in special places, in stillness or when words simply can't capture quite what we've encountered, yet we know something meaningful has happened around or to us.

- *A sense of holiness* – These are moments when we experience feeling close to God. We recognise him in close proximity to us through profound experiences and places that give us 'a sense of the Holy, a sense of that which holds all things together, a sense of God'.

- *Holiness and justice* – This speaks of a desire to be people of justice, whose resources are shared fairly. We long for people to have safe places to live and enough food to eat, and we offer a welcome to strangers and the lonely.

- *Walking the path together* – This reflects John Wesley's firmly held belief that faith is best worked out in community with each other. We have a sense of travelling through life with others, sharing the joys and difficulties as we seek to be truthful and compassionate.

- *Holy living* – This is about adopting a different way of life, where we can live out trust in God, asking for his help and committing to making a difference to the world we find ourselves in. These become habits that, once embedded in our lives, reflect the glory and wonder of our creator God.

These offer us some superb starting points for thinking about how we embed concepts of holiness into our everyday experiences as families. Holiness is about actively choosing to live God's way rather than our own way. It speaks of how we meet and engage with God, worship him and grow in discipleship as we walk a life of faith alongside others of all ages. Have you ever considered that we might as families indeed be called to live as 'holy huddles' – not in the exclusive sense but in the sense that our families welcome others to be family with us and that we live with an attitude that a holy home is one in pursuit of God, who dwells there? What an exciting adventure to embark upon!

The theme of growing in holiness as family is continued in the words of the prophet Micah, later in the Old Testament:

> No, O people, the Lord has told you what is good,
>   and this is what he requires of you:
> to do what is right, to love mercy,
>   and to walk humbly with your God.
> MICAH 6:8

Here is the covenant made between God and his people. Alongside a deepening relationship with God, households demonstrate their faithfulness through their lifestyle and through applying this to how they engage in the world around them. This verse presents a valuable guide to the features of a holy life – doing what is right, loving mercy and walking humbly with God are to be the hallmarks of a family walking in fellowship together. Faith foundations are built at home, and parents have a vital role in modelling and integrating them into a daily lived experience for all family members. This builds 'congruity between a faith that is professed and a faith that is practiced. It means showing in life and deed that faith matters'.[38]

The previous two verses in Micah invite us to consider the question of what we can offer to God:

> What can we bring to the Lord?
>   Should we bring him burnt offerings?
> Should we bow before God Most High
>   with offerings of yearling calves?
> Should we offer him thousands of rams
>   and ten thousand rivers of olive oil?
> Should we sacrifice our firstborn children
>   to pay for our sins?
> MICAH 6:6–7

What is it that God expects of us? To bring him our sacrifices? Can we somehow repay what he has done for us or provide compensation for our wrongdoing? No, it's simply not possible. These are not the ways in which God longs to see us respond. Instead we find ourselves compelled to do what is right, to love mercy and to walk humbly with him.

In other words, make choices in life that respect others. Cultivate attitudes of helpfulness and kindness. Demonstrate compassion and grace. Be ready to forgive. Let generosity be an everyday marker of how we steward our resources. Be prayerful people who read and engage with scripture, experiencing God's presence, not solely storing up head knowledge of him but embracing a willingness to let him mould and change us.

This is what a life of doing right, loving mercy and walking humbly looks like. And it can be a wonderful approach to nurturing holiness at home in our attitudes and values. Are these things intertwined with how we build relationships with each other? Do we model them in our interactions? Do they inform our decision-making? Do we place God at the very centre of the places we dwell in?

The sentiment found in Micah 6 is reflected in John Wesley's statement: 'The gospel of Christ knows of no religion, but social; no holiness but social holiness.'[39] This enhances our understanding of holiness as being very much deeply rooted in our everyday experience. As Andrew Stobart further explains:

> Any holiness that is not thoroughly conversant with its 'social' context is not worthy of the name. Holiness is always a lived entity, generated within the community of Christ, but also informed by and worked out within the cultural structures that provide definition to our daily lives. The gospel of Christ knows of no holiness but holiness within contemporary culture.[40]

So holiness seems an entirely useful word to apply when we're considering how families might grow in faith – something that occurs between family members dwelling as a household – and yet also as they go out and live their daily lives. A holistic approach to life and faith then creates the environment where family discipleship flourishes, in a community that provides support and care for all.

2 Trinity as family

Recently the doctrine of the Trinity has increasingly been informing family theology. It offers a wealth of insights that enable us to imagine a dynamic and interactive paradigm for ministry with parents, children and the wider family. As Scott Hahn asserts, 'God is not like a family. He is a family.'[41] The understanding of God as three persons in one – possessing an identity as individuals, each with distinct roles and purposes, combined in divine nature and sharing characteristics – provides a lens through which we can gain new perceptions of how families function and relate. And while the three are one, the one is also three separate entities.

In Theology and Families, Thatcher presents a contemporary theology of the Trinity that firmly places families and children at the centre, an approach that recognises God's nature to be 'a loving community of persons',[42] who exist in relationship with and for one another. Our identity as family, he asserts, is best understood through drawing together a person's individual uniqueness with how he or she socially relates to others. Authentic family is where separate persons find their purpose in loving care for each other, serving another's needs, without individual members having priority over another. Relationship is key! A Trinitarian theology of family places love in relation to others as a vital feature – indeed it's impossible to love without being in relationship. This is divine love in action – unconditional love is mutually demonstrated among the persons of the Trinity, who invite families to participate in the wonder and joy of also being loved. These relationships have 'elements of covenant, grace, empowerment, and intimacy as family members strive to maintain their unique individuality within family unity'.[43] Members of a family are gifts for and to one another, to be loved and to reciprocate the love offered. It's here we can glimpse God's divine purpose in creating us as family – not primarily to benefit ourselves but to be ever concerned with and preferring those in our family.

Viewing family life from a Trinitarian perspective can be especially powerful when considering hurting families. Families can be destructive and harmful environments, where control, blame and rejection are the features of daily life. God's desire for family is altogether different. Daniel Migliore's definition of the Trinity is invaluable: 'wonderous divine love that freely gives of itself to others and creates community, mutuality, and shared life. God creates and relates to the world this way because this is the way God is eternally God.'[44]

Here is a template for family life, built on principles of generosity, relation-ship, empathy and collective participation. Through more effective communication and growing an understanding of what covenant family is, Balswick and Balswick believe, transformation can be possible and relationships go from 'hurting to healing' as maturity develops.[45]

God shapes us through our interactions with others, a strong biblical theme picked up by Steven Emery-Wright and Ed Mackenzie: 'We are created for others, and we find life not in isolation but in relating to those around us.'[46] Through the struggles and challenges encountered in our family lives – from adjusting to life with a newborn, to launching teenagers and young adults into life beyond the home, to providing care and support for ageing relatives – we discover God at work. Our relationships can be deepened and enhanced if we welcome the opportunity for our characters to be honed and redefined as life unfolds.

A theology of family based on the Trinity offers a refreshing shift from focusing on family structure, particularly that of the nuclear family (often disproportionately held up as the ideal). A Trinitarian approach offers life-enhancing scope for many differing forms of contemporary family, as it emphasises modes and features of effective functioning rather than prioritising composition of members. Families can draw strength from embracing 'the interdependence of working together for the good of the whole',[47] which affirms the contribution everyone makes, helping them to generate a family identity shared by all.

3 Jesus-shaped family

The New Testament offers what could be called a 'gospel of family' as observed through the life and ministry of Jesus: a theology rooted in how Jesus interacted with people from diverse backgrounds and in a variety of circumstances as well as rooted in the breadth of his teaching.

Through his words and actions, Jesus offered abundant insights into how full and transformative family life could be. In this dynamic paradigm, it's possible to envisage a theology that embraces all kinds of family, giving them a place that intentionally draws them into new encounters with the divine.

So much of Jesus' ministry and interaction was countercultural. (Indeed, it could be argued that all he did was!) He recognised what it meant to be an outsider, excluded from the usual settings of public power and discourse. He knew that new routes into fullness of life wouldn't be found in the accepted places. He understood what it was like to exist outside of societal norms, and he actively pursued an incarnational life with people and places in those contexts. This speaks to us of God seeing through those humanly created structures and processes that become barriers to relationship with him. Through Jesus, God redefines what it means to know him and be known by him. All can come.

We see this in a host of different encounters with people from varied backgrounds, cultures, experiences and beliefs. In the parable of the good Samaritan (Luke 10), we are urged to stop and take notice instead of passing by, to meet people's needs, regardless of who they are, instead of being guided by hostility. Here's a man, a despised foreigner, in dire need, following a violent and aggressive attack. Yet Jesus asserts that it is this man who is our neighbour, part of our community, and therefore requiring us to respond. We're urged not to ignore our fellow humans but to display compassion, offer help and do what's needed to aid their recovery.

On another occasion, in conversation with a woman at a well, also a Samaritan (John 4), Jesus demonstrates again the need to cross cultural barriers, to not allow accepted norms to obstruct how we engage and care for those we live alongside. Jesus and the woman have a full and frank conversation about her life, the marker of their dialogue being grace – grace extended to all, available for all, regardless of status or background. Jesus invites her to accept God's freely given gift to her of living water and, while he references her marital status, this isn't the purpose of speaking with her. He's far more interested in helping her recognise him for who he is, as he replies when she enquires about the coming Messiah, 'I who speak to you am He' (John 4:26, NASB).

Then there's the much more public encounter with Zacchaeus, the infamous tax collector (Luke 19). Intrigued by the rumours of who this Jesus is, Zacchaeus is determined to find out more, and he goes to great lengths to catch a glimpse of Jesus as he passes through Jericho. It would have been simple to keep walking, to head on to his destination, but for Jesus, Zacchaeus is the priority; he is the destination; he's the man Jesus needs to speak honestly with. Despite the muttering that surrounds their meeting, the sidelong glances and looks that say, 'Why on earth would you spend time with *him*?', this is the core of Jesus' calling – to invite those who are excluded, who believe themselves to be on the periphery of 'religious society', for whom access to their loving heavenly Father lies behind a door that's been firmly locked, bolted and sealed.

Through all these instances we see Jesus declaring again and again, 'You're welcome, come in!' It's a gospel of inclusion; no one was considered unworthy of his time or an imposition to his ministry. This was his calling, to reach out to those finding themselves on the periphery, to challenge the accepted view of who was in or out, welcome or unwelcome, worthy or unworthy. Jesus wrecked the religious norms, leaving them in tatters when his life, death and resurrection announced a new covenant. As Thatcher reminds us, Jesus' love is transformative: 'What matters is how Christ's love for them encompasses and redeems them now.'[48] Jesus' love is not for a select few who have mastered how to follow religious rules and regulations but is for anyone willing to take a step of faith in following him.

Home as a place for faith is something Jesus also recognised. Alongside all the necessary household chores and routines of eating, sleeping and raising children, home is a place where faith is nurtured and questioned. Jesus knew the value of meeting people on their own turf, in their own domestic settings – with Zacchaeus, as well as Mary and Martha. He understood home as a place to learn and wrestle with faith. In these stories Jesus recognises the value of being the guest in someone's home, of being invited in. He explicitly tells the disciples to never hesitate to accept hospitality, to bless homes when they enter and to remain there to eat and drink. These are spaces where relationships develop, through everyday rituals such as meals and time spent together. They're places to treasure and value highly.

Yet Jesus reminds us that much of what occupies us at home is a distraction, as he emphasises to Martha: 'There is only one thing worth being concerned about' (Luke 10:42). At the centre of our lives together as family is our devotion to God, to being committed followers regardless of our age or depth of understanding. Home is to be a place where faith flourishes, where it's woven into our way of being with other family members, that has its hallmarks in our relationships with them – an image that reminds us of the command to 'love the Lord your God with all your heart, all your soul, and all your strength' (Deuteronomy 6:5).

There are tensions in the gospels on occasion in Jesus' interactions with his own biological family, which might suggest he was anti-family or dismissive of the role and place of parents and siblings. What are we meant to take from his declaration in Luke 12:53 about bringing division in families, quoting Micah:

> Father will be divided against son
>   and son against father;
> mother against daughter
>   and daughter against mother;
> and mother-in-law against daughter-in-law
>   and daughter-in-law against mother-in-law'

Surely this serves to undermine much else of what he teaches. Is Jesus saying that family shouldn't be important and an essential part of our lives? No, instead he is making a profound statement about the place God occupies in our lives. As Richard Melick Jr points out, 'The Gospels reveal a higher concern than family. The kingdom of God must have top priority.

Even family relationships, as important as they are, should not deter one from fulfilling God's plan.'[49] This is Jesus' point. Family is crucial but God always remains first; as Thatcher describes it, 'Kingdom above kin.'[50]

There were often also instances when Jesus created family for and with others, knowing the importance of those relationships in shaping our ability to thrive in life. Even while enduring the cross, Jesus' concern is for his mother, asking John to care for her once he's no longer around to do so (John 19:26–27). He knows that family is a support network, a place of care, and that we need others, whether or not blood ties exist. The kind of 'new covenant community' advocated by Jesus has open doors to all, 'not on the basis of inheritance and blood ties, but on the basis of active obedience to the will of God'.[51] From a place of knowing and loving our creator, we're enabled and called to love others. Our households are to be ecosystems of love, forgiveness, generosity and welcome, places to belong that operate as family for each other beyond the traditional forms and structures that are often assumed to be the only setting for authentic family experience. A Christ-centred theology is valuable to us, as it presents an alternative paradigm for family to that of the nuclear family with 2.4 children.

Conclusion

These three theological perspectives offer a foundation for our ministry with families. They provide us with a sound basis for all we say and do as we set out to support and care for parents, children and families of all shapes, sizes and backgrounds. By developing our theological thinking, we have the opportunity to imagine fresh and innovative approaches to family ministry, recognising how they are to be interwoven into the very fabric of the work we do and the lives families live. So in summary:

- *Holiness at home* illustrates how family life is the context for our encounter with God, that as we live day to day in community with each other, there is an opportunity for God to speak to us. A holy life is one where justice flows out of a family's actions, who embrace compassion in their interactions with each other, choosing to grow in discipleship that is marked by humility.

- *Trinity as family* offers a template for treasuring family life, recognising that God is family – he exists in relationship as Father, Son and Holy Spirit, three in one and one in three, each freely giving for the sake of the other. Trinitarian approaches to the family are united in a mutual yearning to prefer the other, to seek the best for the other members. This approach adds an authenticity to our interactions as we learn to live better as families, whether or not we are all under the same roof.

- *Jesus-shaped family* introduces the countercultural element of Jesus' ministry, which sought to establish a new covenant. Through welcoming the outsider and those on the periphery, we're able to grasp what it truly means to love God and our neighbour and to recognise the grace-filled invitation God extends to us all.

This theological thinking helpfully directs us to some core ideas in relation to family ministry:

- *Families are to be faithful followers* – our relationships with God are to be lived out not in isolation from each other but rather in the context of our daily family life. Here we can aid each family member's discipleship to flourish 24/7 as we explore questions and learn from one another's experiences. Age is no barrier: from the very young to the very old we influence and encourage other family members to follow God wholeheartedly. There's a place for all to be cheering on others in the family in their pursuit of faith. Finding ways to support families as they do this is a significant question for those working with and ministering to them.

- *The home matters* – what happens behind closed doors as families live day-to-day – the conversations, meals, arguments, laughter, tears and challenges of striving to be family – genuinely matters. How family members relate to each other and are encouraged to build healthy, strong relationships is a core aspect of family ministry and something to be promoted through the activities, programmes and times when everyone gathers together. For families, there is an element of sacrifice in this and a willingness to embrace vulnerability. But resilience at home can grow through recognising that our life as family together matters and needs to be worked at.

- *Family function over structure* – there's a higher value placed on the way a group of people experiences being family for and with each other rather than who the members are and what their relation is. Family can be effectively created in a variety of forms with different members, regardless of status, culture, sexual orientation or background. Children thrive in homes where family functions effectively; their well-being is vastly reduced if this features detrimental behaviours and attitudes. Children are much less impacted by the form of family they find themselves in. There's an urgent need to remove the traditional lens which dictates that family should be a particular structure and to recognise the rich diversity experienced in families today.

- *Inclusivity* – the compelling example and teaching of Jesus remind us to be mindful of those on the fringes; those who feel, for whatever reason, that the church is an exclusive family they could never hope to participate in or be welcomed by; those who, because of their own circumstances or family experience, believe a faith community would never be a place of belonging for 'someone like me'. Our family ministry needs to always be finding ways to be inclusive, helping to create family for those whose experience has been painful or who have little grasp of how life-enhancing it can be.

This is a profound truth: being included, receiving an unconditional welcome to the kingdom of God, is available to all, regardless. Jesus' very presence among us once and for all sweeps away convictions of unworthiness and unacceptance. He demonstrated that God's gracious invitation extends to all families: old and new; related through blood and not; with two parents and with one; with few needs and with deep-seated ones; who struggle to communicate well and who seem to have it all together but behind closed doors are fighting battles no one else is aware of. No family is barred from knowing the transformative nature of the living God.

Theology of this nature releases families from believing that they do not match up, that they fail to reach the 'Christian' bar of what family should be. Flawed and often unfounded notions, that only through being a nuclear family can we ever hope to come close to God or participate in his kingdom, deprive many of experiencing flourishing life and faith. These theological thoughts have the potential to shape a new, vibrant context for ministering and supporting families that offers hope as they seek to create lasting relationships and life together.

Questions for reflection

Spend some time either individually or with your congregation or church leadership considering these questions. Provide space to consider different viewpoints and understandings.

- What are the core features of your own theology of family? Are these evident in the ministry you're involved in?

- What do you find challenging about the three perspectives presented here?

- What aspects of this theology of family do you want to reflect on further?

3

FAMILY MINISTRY TODAY

Introduction

Defining what family ministry is today is not without its challenges. No single succinct definition exists that effectively describes how this work takes place across churches and communities. Due to its multidimensional nature, it is difficult to capture the essence of ministry with families in a way that conveys its purpose and intention. As one interviewee told the *We Are Family* research project:

> There are hundreds of definitions out there. People call it different things and mean different things by it. They call it all-age ministry, intergenerational ministry, family ministry, household ministry, households of faith.[52]

Pinning family ministry down to a soundbite that is widely accepted is probably beyond our reach. Diana Garland describes the term 'family ministry' as a 'catch-all category of programs designed to support persons in their daily activities and relationships',[53] which perhaps is only a partial picture and suggests a 'doing to' model of ministry, where families are merely recipients rather than participants. There are often congregational and spiritual elements to ministry, those aspects which nurture faith formation, as captured in this definition:

> The process of intentionally and persistently realigning a congregation's proclamation and practices so that parents are acknowledged, trained and held accountable as the persons primarily responsible for the discipleship of their children.[54]

The emphasis here is on families developing in faith together in the context of their participation in a church community. This moves us towards a definition of ministry that combines both of these ideas: an approach seeking to support families in their daily lives and relationships as well as nurturing their spiritual development, enabling them to grow in faith together. Approaches to family ministry have recently become much more holistic, striving to integrate a range of support for families' physical and spiritual needs.

For many churches, embracing a broader definition of family ministry isn't straightforward, given how much the context of work with parents and children has changed, which in turn has impacted how they offer practical support to families and encourage them to grow in faith. For example, even just a few years ago the term 'faith at home' would have been alien to many, but now it's a topic of frequent discussion with many church-based workers exploring innovative new ways to aid families in their discipleship.

Historically, family ministry was easier to define, as much of the provision churches made for families was narrowly prescribed, linked to Sunday school and children's religious education, enabling children and young people to spend time with their peers, learn about the Bible and the Christian faith, and get sound moral foundations. More recently churches have widened their programmes, so that the whole family can be involved. At the same time, giving financial or other practical support to families in need has long been a mandate of the church.

There's a growing recognition that working with children or young people in isolation isn't necessarily the best approach. It can be more beneficial to bring different ages and generations together, exploring new ways to engage with each other in church worship and community. It's exciting to see how those in lay ministry are discovering new routes to offer care for the whole family within broader multigenerational settings.

Ultimately, a church can choose to form its own definition of family ministry based on its location, community and context. It's a worthwhile exercise for any church that wants to missionally reach and support families to spend time reflecting on the goals of their own distinct ministry, tailoring a definition that authentically represents the nature of work they're striving to do.

Exploring and finding a definition for family ministry is essential, as it equips us to wrestle with the big questions of what it is and how we understand it. Reflecting on how we do ministry is vital – it forces us to ask 'why'. Why do we do what we do? Why do we work with these families and not others? Why do we pour our resources, time and energy into these activities and not those? These are the questions that bring us face-to-face with the intentions of our work, things we may not often think about. It is easy to jump in and embark on a host of family ministry activities without giving much thought to the shape of it, what the ultimate aims are or what we hope it might achieve. That approach is fraught with danger, as it can lead to nothing we do being joined up or related to other areas of work. For our ministry to be sustainable and to make an impact, we need to carefully reflect on these questions and be better informed about what's happening locally. Churches are then in a stronger position to be strategic – to plan and implement ministry that is going to make a difference to the lives of the families in their congregations and beyond.

Despite the challenges of keeping pace with how family ministry has been evolving, recently there has been some valuable thinking and research done, which has been hugely helpful in growing our understanding of how ministry to and with families is being approached. Let's look at some of these now.

Approaches to family ministry

In their chapter in *A Theology for Family Ministries*, Timothy Paul Jones and Randy Stinson present three contemporary models that capture recent developments in family ministry. As they point out, these 'represent a break from the segmented-programmatic approaches that dominated twentieth-century churches',[55] that is, when church life was frequently characterised by the separation of generations and age groups and ministry was targeted to particular interests or styles of worship and participation. Instead, the contemporary models place Christian formation at the centre of ministry activity, with the goal of equipping parents to actively create environments where the whole family's faith flourishes.

- *The family-based model* takes an intergenerational approach, while keeping peer-group activities occurring alongside those designed for the whole congregation to participate in. There's an intentionality to gather everyone and prioritise the role of the family as faith is being formed. It's an approach pioneered by Mark DeVries in the context of youth work, who states, 'We try to point as much of our programming as possible in the direction of giving kids and adults excuses to interact together.'[56]

- *The family-integrated model* moves ministry away from a silo model to one of full family integration across church life. Here, all age-specific programmes are removed, enabling everyone to actively grow in faith and understanding together. In this radical model, the home is the hub of ministry activity, providing mutual support and reaching out missionally to other parents and children. It's an approach built on the idea of being a community that exists as a 'family of families'.

- *The family-equipping model* has parents in the ministry spotlight, providing a programme of activity that seeks to train and involve them as the primary disciple-makers of their children. It's an approach that sees the church and home working in partnership to nurture the faith of children and young people. Church life is oriented around this priority so that, although separate age-specific programmes continue, they are restructured to ensure priority is given to equipping parents in this responsibility.

Jones and Stinson are writing from an American perspective, so the lens through which they observe and respond to work with families is different from the UK. Yet much of what they offer for consideration is constructive and beneficial here. For Jones and Stinson, recognising the imperfections of these models is important; no single approach will accomplish all our goals or provide straightforward solutions to the challenges of working with families. Yet all three display principles that underpin ministry with them. They describe these as 'perennial truths':

1 God has called parents to take personal responsibility for the Christian formation of their children;
2 the generations need one another;
3 family ministry models must be missional.

These characteristics can be a valuable starting point for conversations around the nature of our ministry to families. We can ask ourselves where they sit in our priorities and how we might therefore embed them into the structures of church life. The models suggested here recognise the importance of adopting an approach to ministry as opposed to simply implementing a programme. There's an essential distinction to be made between the two, as it can often be the case that giving time and space to considering the principles that underpin ministry is overlooked in our haste to establish a project or embark on the practical work of ministry. We'll return to this later in the book.

It would be fascinating to rate our family ministry (say, giving it a score out of ten) based on those three truths offered above. Is our work with families supportive of parents as they seek to create Christian households? Where are the connecting points for different generations? Is there enough emphasis on shaping a missional ministry? Would our scores be high or low? Sometimes it can be good to ask the tough questions, and if we don't have an answer we could do some further thinking, inviting others to join us as we do so.

The Family Ministry Research Project

The influential Family Ministry Research Project captured much of these recent developments in its report *We Are Family*. Following a broad study and investigation across Britain, the project presented a comprehensive picture of all that is taking place in churches. Based on data gathered from church-based workers from a range of denominations, along with telephone interviews, surveys and a review of job descriptions, the research project compiled rich information of how families are engaged in church life and receive support through a host of different groups and channels.

The study indicated that family ministry occurs in many contexts and places with a wide variety of families. Participation varies depending on the nature of the activity, but over time, the report showed, many churches built strong relationships with parents, children, young people and grandparents through the services provided. For instance, if a family takes part in a church toddler group, there is a stronger likelihood they will be willing and keen to join in other church activities.

One of the significant drivers for churches wanting to embark on work with families is the rising age of congregations. There is often a hope that family work will attract a younger demographic, bringing a new lease of life into the church. Family workers employed in these circumstances shared some of the challenges this brought, particularly in terms of evaluating their work if Sunday morning services didn't see an increase in family engagement. Finding ways to measure the effectiveness of ministry was one of the challenges they faced. There could be a host of wonderful support and provision available that families valued, but this was rarely considered by their churches to be a measure of success. It continues to be a point of frustration for many family workers employed by churches that better systems are not in place to gauge the value of their ministry, reflecting the dynamic nature of all they do.

Asserting a presence in the local community was another driver identified by the research project. Family workers who took part in the day-long consultation events shared many examples of ways in which they had a presence beyond church buildings into their local neighbourhood, often working with schools, nurseries and children's centres. Family workers are often well known in their local vicinity, recognised by parents and children who had come into contact with them via church-based activities. This raises the profile of church groups and services, giving a sense of connection to the wider community and building the church's reputation as people and places providing care and a welcome. Effective church-based family work places a high value on becoming embedded into community life and embracing the principle of being 'in the world'. Many family-work practitioners invest heavily in growing these local relationships, which frequently bear fruit when establishing new projects or programmes. Being rooted in the neighbourhood was a value many workers shared.

In terms of the breadth of work taking place, the study captured the extensive sweep of family ministry being delivered in cities, towns and villages across the UK. These were focused into two strands: *ministry*, the activities that contain a spiritual or faith-based element, and *support*, activities that seek to provide pastoral care or practical help.

Ministry centres on those activities with a missional edge, that explore ways to grow faith and discipleship, that find routes into being more intergenerational and that emphasise equipping households to be places of faith nurture and growth. So when we're talking 'ministry' as family-work practitioners, this concerns the way in which families develop spiritually in prayer, in worship and in their knowledge and understanding of scripture and Christian life. It can also mean how they're engaged in evangelistic activity, becoming confident transmitters of the gospel in the places they move and work and learn. Part of a practitioner's role can be to draw attention to the spiritual encounters in everyday life, bringing those faith thoughts from the fringe to centre stage. As mentioned by one interviewee about some of the families they encountered, 'Faith is a blip in the horizon of their lives, which doesn't mean that there isn't any spirituality in their lives, there may be, but those families are not necessarily part of the faith community.'[57]

A theme of the practitioner discussions was that people want to talk about 'big questions' around life and spirituality, but they no longer turn to the church for answers. So in some settings creating authentic new forums in which to host faith conversations is vital if families are to engage meaningfully with the Christian faith. As one family worker stated:

The numbers of families who are interested is definitely growing. But… bringing them further into the church and bringing them further to the core of what we're about… seems to be the big sticking point at the moment.[58]

Exploring faith, and fostering it so that it develops further and incorporates families into church life, appears to be a key aspect of ministry for many workers. Practitioners are committed to the lifelong work of nurturing disciples and know it to be the systematic, day-in-day-out of relational involvement that can be life-changing for many parents and children.

Support activities are primarily community-focused. They provide opportunities to build relationships with people, have a strong thread of social action running through them and involve working with local partners. Provision can be in a variety of forms but often has at its core a desire to enhance families' general well-being, whether on a practical basis or improving emotional and mental health.

Much of what takes place under the umbrella of family support has high regard for hospitality and welcome: endeavouring for activities and groups to be places where families can participate authentically, receiving a genuine invite in without pressure to conform or subscribe to a particular set of beliefs at the outset. This is an important value for family workers, and many testified to the difference it had made for many they met who had previously felt on the fringe, excluded or beyond the apparent perimeter of church life and involvement.

Meeting local need through social action enterprise was very evident in the kind of support churches engaged in. Faith in action is what people were alluding to when talking about food banks, providing furniture or clothing for families in need, churches being embedded in local networks alongside children's centres and other secular partners in the community, and providing a safety net for the poor, vulnerable and elderly from all communities in the neighbourhood of the church. Investing in this work is seen as a key expression of faith, part of what Jesus called his followers to actively pursue in terms of loving our neighbours. Following a raft of funding cuts in the wake of austerity, the church has become in some places the 'last man standing' as families are adversely affected by the scaling down and closing of local authority services. Plugging this gap has been an observed trend by many practitioners in cities, towns and villages across the UK. As one worker stated, the church has an important role here in the current context:

> There's a lot of families out there that we know about that have real problems… the social workers and the people out there, there's not many at the moment and children's centres are being cut. There's a place there that maybe the church could step in, because it's a worrying time at the minute.[59]

Providing practical support and signposting to other local services, agencies and charities featured among the activities churches invested in to meet need in their local contexts.

While the two strands, ministry and support, are helpful in defining the work taking place, they represent a false division, as all that's been described can be argued to be ministry. If we take a holistic view of what it means to minister to families, then everything a church provides, from a listening ear and drop-in advice sessions to social events and services which nurture faith, is in some shape and form ministry.

In many settings toddler groups are a good example of how churches seek to bring elements of their ministry and support together in one expression. Such groups have often been at the heart of provision to parents and young children, and in many instances family ministry has grown out of these groups, which have been the backbone of community activity. It's believed that around 55% of churches in England run toddler groups, and many have a close connection to the hosting congregation. Since the turn of the century, there's been a move away from calling these 'mother and toddler' groups, in recognition of the shifting nature of family life. Many groups welcome a wider variety of caring adults, including grandparents, nannies, childminders and foster carers. For all these people, as well as mums and dads, the group can be a place of indispensable support and contact with others. The Toddler Project reflected this, as it heard of the importance of making adults and children feel welcomed, comfortable and able to fully integrate into group activities. It highlighted five areas that are primarily seen as missional opportunities for groups:

- Love and serve young families
- Be distinctively Christian
- Nurture faith journeys
- Build the church community
- Support toddler group leaders[60]

As groups become more diverse, there's a need to consider what appropriate types of care and support may be valuable. Grandparents will have different needs to childminders. Ensuring that toddler groups remain settings accessible to all may have its challenges in the future. As increasing numbers of parents are in employment, there's an inevitable impact on how toddler groups operate. Group leaders may be elderly and finding volunteers to join teams is difficult, so new approaches to running them need to be explored.

Within this mix of new expressions of care, faith and support, it's impossible to ignore the significant impact of Messy Church (**messychurch.org.uk**), a way of being church that seeks to gather families and people of all ages to create communities of faith outside of Sunday services. These worship spaces offer opportunities to encounter God in refreshing, new and dynamic ways, through creative activities, storytelling and a mealtime that gathers everyone around the table. Messy Church has offered a warm welcome for many who previously considered themselves not to be the sort of people who go to church or who never imagined it had anything to offer them. It has ushered in a new era for church life that actively seeks to engage authentically with people where they are and provide space to ask questions and nurture friendships. Children's, youth and family ministries have all been impacted to some degree by how Messy Church has flourished, raising questions about deeper faith development and discipleship and how best to include young people.

Across these different expressions of family ministry, it's practitioners who lead the way in shaping provision and meeting the needs of families in congregations and local communities. Their roles are rarely identical and contain a range of what might be seen as competing responsibilities and tasks. For some the 'family worker' role has been a natural extension of children's and youth ministry, recognising that these groups don't exist in isolation. For others it's been a bolt-on to an existing specialism. This blurring of roles has been seen in some respects as a worrying trend, with the potential for specific skills and knowledge to become lost in the broader field of ministry with families.

The range of work being done by family workers who participated in the *We Are Family* survey illustrates the competing/complementary strands of family work. From hands-on activities with a specific age group, such as leading Sunday school, to mixed-aged provision, such as Messy Church, to admin tasks and practical duties, practitioners' jobs are vast. Preparations for imminent events or sessions and finding ways to involve volunteers in teamwork were often high on their to-do lists. Managing their broad workload was challenging for many who felt on occasion that supervision was lacking. Putting processes in place that support family workers to be effective in their planning and delivery is vital in order for them to flourish in ministry. Yet there's little evidence currently that those in lay ministry have access to healthy, accountable oversight that values their personal well-being and development alongside the drive to bring greater numbers of families into the life of the church.

When it comes to training, the *We Are Family* research project indicates that practitioners were usually sent on short workshops or one-day conferences that emphasised practical skills rather than theological understanding and strategic thinking about ministry. As such, while the training workers undertook was usually effective and valuable, and offered much-needed networking opportunities, it didn't provide a context for deeper professional development. As family ministry continues to unfold and become more established, it is vital to ensure that practitioners are effectively prepared and equipped for the work they do. Enabling family workers to be strategic thinkers and willing to share experience and knowledge within communities of practice will contribute hugely to ongoing innovation in this field.

Embedding family ministry within the wider mission and work of the church is also key, as in some settings it has become the sole responsibility of a paid worker. That work with families is no longer an enterprise for the whole church to contribute to and join in, being instead tasked to a professional, has been seen as a relinquishing of the church's primary community-building role. The impact of this is seen in a host of ways, not least in the fact that family workers feel isolated and unsupported, but also in that clear routes for families to become woven into the wider life of the church simply don't exist. Rediscovering a corporate sense of missional life and faith shared by everyone is a key aim for those in family ministry and leadership roles.

Conclusion

From this whistle-stop tour of the current landscape of family work in Britain, there are trends worth highlighting. These are helpfully summarised by the *We Are Family* research project in their findings as follows:

- *Understanding family ministry* – Recognising that family has changed significantly influences the way we work with them. The nuclear family no longer represents the ideal or lived experience for many households across the UK, and giving careful thought to how we therefore approach offering support is vital if ministry is to be relevant. There needs to be greater attention paid to the types of families found in a church's neighbourhood, their lifestyles and their livelihoods, so that ministry is better tailored to their needs.

- *The spectrum of family ministry* – This requires us to develop new understanding that work with families takes many varied forms. Some of it is very practical in nature, providing relational support and enabling families to thrive, particularly during significant life-stage transitions (e.g. adjusting to the arrival of a newborn baby, blending two families to become a new one, nurturing teenage independence or caring for elderly relatives) as well as when encountering troublesome life events or issues. Other aspects of the work contain a spiritual dimension, having a distinct missional edge, seeking to provide opportunities to explore questions of faith and what it means to be a follower of Jesus.

- *Issues in family ministry and support* – There is a range of related questions identified by the research. It reflects that young families, often participating in Messy Church and toddler groups, are part of what's been termed the 'missing generation' (those who have had no or little contact with church). They bring a range of differing ideas and understandings about the Christian faith, so it can't be assumed they will relate to the rituals and language used in church life. There's a need to consider where the routes into working intergenerationally are and how different age groups are brought together in worship and grow to be community with one another. Another issue identified was the value of exploring routes into partnerships with other agencies and charities working locally and how these could be mutually beneficial for both churches and the families they know and work with.

- *Equipping for family ministry* – From the breadth of work taking place in churches across the UK, it's clear that there is often a lack of strategic planning for ministry activity. Finding ways to combat this scattergun approach is essential to make best use of resources, as is undertaking education and training of those in lay ministry. Many church-based workers had received minimal training, and they expressed a strong desire to be better equipped for their work and ministry.

These four findings provide a frank and defined essential starting point for further reflection on how we can intentionally shape family ministry in the 21st century. Addressing these areas will enable our work to flourish and to be authentic, relevant and life-enhancing for the families we work with. *We Are Family* pinpointed some significant developments in family ministry, but it also raised questions about how our work could be more effective. If family ministry is going to become embedded across the life of the church as a source of community for families, we need to get serious in our strategy and thinking. It's no longer acceptable to assume that any work is better than no work; we need to be intentional in the way we approach and sustain ministry. Shaping activities so that they fit the lives and kinds of contemporary family that exist today is key, yet the church hasn't recognised the change that's been taking place over recent decades. Is our work rooted in the current societal context? There needs to be a shift of focus from family structure to family function, which invests in relationships, creating an environment in which each family can flourish. Do we take a holistic approach, combining the two strands of ministry and support, or do we see practical support as being at odds with nurturing faith? What if families encountered caring support in the church that valued their whole being, seeking to entwine gospel love with meeting their physical need? This is a transformational picture of ministry that could impact families of all kinds and have a lasting influence on their interactions with each other, those they live alongside and the God who created them.

Questions for reflection

The *We Are Family* report posed 15 key questions for leaders and those working with families based on the four major findings.[61] These remain vital questions for reflection when setting out on any kind of family ministry. Choose a set of questions or an area for you to consider further.

Understanding family ministry

- What are the various types of family found in your local context or community?

- How could family work and ministry in your context become more inclusive of different kinds of family?

- How does your context impact on your priorities for family work? What is the profile of the local population?

The spectrum of family ministry

- Which elements of family work are a priority in your church?

- What are the drivers behind the work being done with families? What do you hope to achieve?

- How do churches achieve a balance between responding to need and missional activity?

- What opportunities exist in the church and local context for family workers to engage in wider, more strategic discussions about ministry?

Issues in family ministry and support

- How are leaders in the church being trained and equipped to support ministry for all generations?

- How does the whole church community come together for shared worship and conversation? What would need to change to make this happen?

- What impact have funding cuts on local services had in your area?

- How well connected are workers and volunteers with local agencies that support families?

- Who are the key local partners in family ministry and support?

Equipping for family ministry

- What structures does the church have to enable it to manage, support and train volunteers?

- What training can be offered to more fully equip those working with families, including study to develop theological approaches to family work?

- What does effective supervision look like that provides both account-ability and support for family workers?

II

SEVEN HABITS FOR HIGHLY EFFECTIVE FAMILY MINISTRY

Having explored the theory and theology of family ministry today, we now, in the second part of this guide, reflect on the values and habits required for effective family ministry. These principles and practices are central to how we construct ministry. They determine our approach, offering us the means to build support, care and wider provision on a solid foundation that will meet the needs of families in significant ways.

While considering how to apply what follows in the coming chapters, bring the features of your individual setting to mind. Ask yourself, 'What is it like where I serve and work?' In this way, you can imagine working in a relevant and authentic way. Giving time and space for meaningful reflection will enable these habits to be embedded in your own practice in the church, community and beyond.

4

BE STRATEGIC

Introduction

As much as I am a loud and proud advocate for ministry with families, in recent times I'm increasingly inclined to insert the word 'strategic' before 'ministry'. Working with families is essential in church life, but if it's not underpinned by solid principles and strategy, the chances of it making a long-term difference to those families are minimal. 'Strategy' has often been a dirty word in Christian circles – it can seem at odds with being God-led or Spirit-inspired – but it has the potential to transform the way we approach ministry. It can clarify otherwise vague aims and intentions, and it can help us allocate resources more effectively.

Many of the services and programmes we offer in church can be aimed at a wide range of parents, children and extended families. Indeed, they may not be targeted to a specific audience at all but instead be offered to anyone who's interested. Through adopting more strategic practices, these activities can be fine-tuned, becoming more relevant to those families participating in the ministry and support offered.

There is value at this point in noting one of the most significant strategic programmes for families that I have witnessed: Sure Start. Launched in 1998, Sure Start is a UK government initiative seeking to transform the lives of early-years families. It is a prime example of what can be accomplished when taking a strategic approach to family support. It was a radical policy – further developed in 2003 as part of the Every Child Matters agenda – which set out to tackle family poverty and reach families on the fringes of society, going beyond addressing financial need to combat social exclusion, reform childcare and improve access to work.

Through establishing children's centres in the 20 most deprived areas of the UK, Sure Start sought to bring a range of local health, education and support services all under one roof. As Angela Anning and Mog Ball reflect: 'The Sure Start intervention took this holistic approach to raising the life chances of young children, nested in families, in turn nested in whole communities, as its starting point.'[62] One of Sure Start's aims was to build stronger families by reducing the barriers between them and support services. There was a desire to 'reshape services: to make them more flexible and responsive to local demographics and priorities'. In other words, to be the 'glue that would bind together a range of local services' and make available what was needed by families in their vicinity.

The programme's ambition was huge – a £500 million investment in reforming the way services to children and families were provided over a ten-year period. Opinions vary widely on how successful it was, but early evaluations suggested some significant benefits, such as changes in parental behaviour and improved relationships with those considered hardest to reach. Yet it was apparent that with such challenging goals, ten years would never be long enough to bring about the changes hoped for. The National Evaluation of Sure Start concluded by being 'cautiously positive', but it remained sceptical that the programme significantly accomplished what it set out to do. Anecdotally, through its dedicated local approach, Sure Start did make a great impact on families and improved their ability to function well as households.

The way Sure Start approached working with families – taking a strategic view to base services locally and attempting to provide these holistically – speaks into the way support can be offered through churches. Churches are already well placed to be hubs of local care and support for those living nearby, so we do well to consider how best to meet the needs of the families we know in ways that reflect our mission and calling as God's people.

Ministry with families often presents a wealth of opportunity, and deciding how to approach this work can be challenging, but having a strategy is a valuable starting point. In Families at the Center of Faith Formation', John Roberto defines strategy as 'a careful plan or method for achieving a particular goal, usually over a long period of time'.[63] We're not talking short-term gain here; instead we should be looking at ways to intentionally respond, making a significant impact on the lives of parents, children and the wider family.

In this chapter we'll explore:

* family ministry within the context of the church's wider mission;
* approaches to family ministry that take a strategic view across the entirety of church life;
* becoming reflective practitioners who are able to assess the impact these approaches could have on the families we know and work with, as well as recognising the importance of our own ongoing professional development.

Being strategic

During the *We Are Family* research project, it became clear that family ministry was so often approached in a 'doing it all' way. Many churches, faced with a wealth of opportunities for service that they were itching to take, set out to offer a host of different groups, activities, courses, drop-ins – whatever seemed a good idea at the time. This was reflected in the broad job descriptions of family workers and in the diverse activities they were expected to lead, and it indicates the lack of clarity that continues to exist around family ministry. Family ministry is difficult to define unless we take steps to identify priorities at the outset. This was often a response to the cry of congregations, 'We have no families', and accompanied with an air of desperation.

There is also a need for church leadership, lay workers and congregations to share the same ethos on family ministry. What often happens, however, is that it is outsourced, 'the common view being that churches tend to think anything new needs an expert, or that anything outside general ministry should be delivered by an expert in that field'.[64]

Diana Garland believes that the most effective model of leadership in family ministry is one of whole-church collaboration:

Family ministry leaders, then, are not primarily the ones doing family ministry; instead they are the ones who remind, call to collaboration and orchestrate the leadership of others in the diversity of the church's activities and programs.[65]

So those in family ministry roles are there to galvanise and coordinate all efforts working towards shared aims and principles, not necessarily to be the experts who know and can do it all. They're central figures who need to be thinking strategically, inviting the wider church into the conversation about mission purpose and plans.

Four dangers

When embarking upon family ministry activity, there are four dangers we need to be alert to: jumping in; the programme cure-all; disregarding the families; making it complex

Jumping in

Aesop's fable of the hare and the tortoise, in which the hare sets off at speed with only the goal of winning the race in mind, has plenty of relevant lessons for how (not) to embark on ministry. Observing the wealth of opportunity available on the church doorstep can drive us to immediately leap into action, striving to engage with families in myriad ways – whether in congregational life or missionally out in the community. Resources and efforts end up being thinly spread, and those in family ministry roles attempt to coordinate and oversee everything, but it often results in a scattergun approach, without a great deal of forethought given to whether what is being done was actually required, requested or making a difference.

At the outset it's vital not to overlook an exploration and critique of the reasons for what we intend to do. Proper time and reflection need to be given to establishing the ethos that underpins ministry, considering the specific outcomes we're working towards. Ensuring ministry has a contextual basis before jumping in is essential.

The programme cure-all

Timothy Paul Jones has talked about the 'programmatic cure-all'[66] – the appeal of seeking to find a quick fix, which more often than not leads to a flurry of family-friendly activity that soon fades into the background when the next quick fix arrives on the scene. It's often assumed that adopting an off-the-shelf programme is the most effective response to the array of family ministry opportunities. In reality, no programme will achieve exactly what we want it to – it may in some instances give us some good ideas and form the basis for a specific piece of work with families, but it's not going to meet the wider requirements.

Instead the effectiveness of our family ministry is more dependent on the model we adopt that underpins how we approach what we do. This influences how we engage with families and enables us to always return to the features of the model to guide us when embarking on new aspects of ministry.

Disregarding the families

It seems counterintuitive that we would set out to offer support to and missionally engage with families without considering what they need, but meaningful consultation is often overlooked. A 'good idea' presents itself, and quickly we assign resources and put plans in place to make it happen without giving due consideration to the views of the families we know.

At the outset it's crucial to consider the kinds of families in our neighbourhood. Knowing our context is key: understanding the community we're in from a geographical, economic, social, employment and cultural perspective. Building our knowledge of who lives there, their lifestyle, how they function as family and the challenges they face is all crucial information to grasp before even considering the ways we may be able to work with them.

If we overlook the need to engage with individual families, build relationships with them and learn what may be most helpful for them, what we then offer probably won't be fit for purpose. We need to create relevant and authentic ways, both formal and informal, of consulting with families, to help build this knowledge.

Churches would do well to adopt a 'family advocate' approach, where a group within a congregation actively works on behalf of families – an approach built on all that's known of local families, firmly grounded in the context they're in. It may sound obvious, but families need to be at the core of our thinking and planning for family ministry.

Making it complex

According to Garland, 'the heart of family ministry involves living our life as a congregation in ways that develop and nurture the relationships of families caring for one another and ministering in their communities and world. In some ways this seems a simple way to do family ministry.'[67] Yet she goes on to say that 'simplicity… is sometimes a characteristic most difficult to achieve'.

So often we overcomplicate ministry. In order to meet the needs of families, to provide a broad and varied ministry programme, we add a wealth of activities, each with a specific goal or group in mind. This is always a danger when we don't adopt a strategic approach, finding ourselves unrelentingly bolting on more and more until churches and workers eventually find they're bowing under the weight of it all and the pressure to keep it all going. Complexity can often result in unsustainability – a great burden placed on all those involved that sadly leads to burnout.

Not being afraid to keep it simple, to invest time, resources and energy in key ministry activities, is a radical approach but one that might allow for longevity and greater fruitfulness of all those participating. It also means making tough decisions about *not* doing certain things and accepting the practical limitations that can often exist.

Taking a strategic approach

Developing a strategy needs to be the basis for the practical outworking of ministry with families. When we're faced with a multitude of opportunities and possibilities, it can aid our focus, helping us be more targeted in our approach. As the basis for exploring what this could look like, identifying our guiding principles can helpfully establish the foundations for all we do. These may look different depending on our location and families, but they will always influence the kinds of activity we opt to pursue.

There's been a distinct lack of thinking done on how to approach family ministry strategically and the principles that form the foundation for ministry. What has been done is usually from an American context, which can be problematic to translate to the UK. Diana Garland has possibly given this field the most reflection, and she suggests four principles to underpin family ministry:

● Form, strengthen and disciple families as one focus of everything you do as a church community. This is integrated into all that takes place across the worshipping life of those who gather in fellowship, via Sunday services and beyond into midweek meetings and how families grow in faith together day by day at home.

- Imagine your church programming is a covered wagon: you can only carry so much. Adding more and more activities or groups places a strain that can ultimately hinder the wagon's progress and effectiveness. Being selective in what we take up and engage in leads more often to ministry and people flourishing.

- Provide families with opportunities to be family at church. Recognise that over recent decades there's been an incremental shift to greater separation of families during church gatherings, and there need to be forums for them to come together.

- Build informal, interactive programmes and processes into congregational life. Rather than find new formats to do this, look to create opportunities among what already takes place that will build up, support and encourage families to function well in faith and life.

Note that, rather than zooming into the specifics of family life and need, Garland starts with the life of the congregation. This is a much more holistic perspective of how to approach family ministry. As she states, it's 'helpful to consider family ministry as a perspective we take on congregational life together; it is not just a program… designed with families as the objects of our focus'.[68] This is a significant distinction – our approach to ministering to and supporting families is church-wide, indeed I'd argue community-wide, encompassing all families we interact with. It is an approach to ministry that incorporates therapeutic elements (strengthening how a family functions) alongside nurturing discipleship in the home (strengthening how a family grows in faith) with all who participate.

These principles are helpful as they offer an inclusive approach – they see everyone as being part of the big picture of family work. Families of all kinds – single people (often rarely referenced in relation to family ministry), couples with and without children, multigenerational households – are embraced and encouraged to participate in the church's life. The principles also get away from the silo mentality of seeing family ministry as an isolated specialism; instead they apply family ministry approaches across the congregation and community as a whole. They think intergenerationally.

Strategy starting points

Where do we begin, then, if we want our family ministry activity to be more directed and embedded into the life of churches, families and communities? There are six steps in the process which can guide us to developing a strategic approach to ministry.

1   *Research* – identify the goal. This requires us to consider what we as a church want to achieve, a goal that goes beyond an expressed desire to bring more families into the life of the church. It may not be an isolated aim; rather it may be integrated into the wider missional pursuits of what our church believes we're called to be. At the outset, spending time prayerfully considering God's intention and purposes for us as his people will be tantamount. There needs to be clarity brought to a church's ministry, asking ourselves what we hope it will achieve. Is our goal to equip parents to become more intentional about faith at home? Do we want to create opportunities to explore faith with the families already participating in activities and groups? Do we want to nurture a deeper connection between the different generations of our church and community? Recognising that there are multiple goals while also being willing to limit our vision to a specific one can helpfully clarify our intentions at the outset.

During this stage of exploring our strategic approach, we research people and places to understand the nature of our context and community. We grow our knowledge of who lives nearby, the local geography, the schools and educational institutions within it, where people work, the nature of their working lives, the ebb and flow of day-to-day family life, where and how they spend time with friends. We learn about the cultural composition of the community and the economic challenges it may face. Forming a detailed picture of how our localities function and who populates them places us in a stronger position to know where and what the best starting places for ministry might be.

2   *Pinpoint the priorities* – following an extensive time of research and information gathering, name the priorities. With a breadth of possibility before us, we need to make the tough decisions about the areas we're going to concentrate on. This is a reality check: a chance to assess available resources and decide where to allocate them. If our strategy is to cover a three-to-five-year period, we need to consider what can

be reasonably achieved in the first year and whether there's enough funding/will/impetus to develop this in the coming years. Taking a short-term view isn't helpful – family ministry is a long-term project (some might say a lifetime's work), so beginning with one or two priorities can pave the way to longer-term effectiveness, if they gather momentum and ensure that firm foundations are built for the future.

3   *Develop strategy* – formulate the plan. This is taking our blue-sky thinking from the shiny version of the future we're hoping for and recognising there are steps that will take us from here to there. It's about moving from the *what* (the stated aim) to the *how* (the map that will get us moving in that direction). Planning can often begin with a core group of individuals who have a passion in this area of ministry. Gathering those individuals together at the outset invites contributions from a range of perspectives. As well as welcoming their professional know-how, it brings a diversity of family experience, which is invaluable when thinking about being both missionally and practically supportive of a range of families.

This is the stage to take the wealth of knowledge we've accrued and identify how our family ministry activity can be designed to best fit our context and those we want and/or need to engage with. A warning: don't create a plan that tries to do it all at once – share the gospel, provide pastoral support, meet profound need and develop disciples on a lifelong exploration of faith! It's worth saying here and now – it's an impossible dream. (Of course, if yours is the one church which magnificently manages to do it all effectively, please don't hesitate to get in touch and share your secret!)

Generating a plan requires working with others in church – those in leadership, volunteers and colleagues – so that the principles we've adopted can be applied to and underpin all we do with families, regardless of where it occurs in church life, whether participating in toddler group, joining in a Harvest service, seeking support with housing issues, establishing Messy Church, offering care to parents of newborns, helping teenagers and parents have healthy relationships, providing spaces for grandparents to spend time with grandchildren, and so on. It's possible to apply our strategic thinking across a host of different settings. Taking a collaborative approach to formulating the plan encourages everyone to share ownership of what's to come.

4   *Communication* – share the outcomes. Once we've established the shape and route of the plan, find a way to communicate it widely across church life, with congregations and families. Deciding what, how and where to do this will depend on individual churches, but it's worth embarking upon a comprehensive time of communicating our goals, priorities and strategy to accomplish them. There may be a host of different forums within which to do this that allow for some Q and A, prayerful reflection and exploration of our family ministry intentions. Creating spaces to do this well is vital, and finding innovative approaches that allow the strategy to be explored in ways besides reading wordy documents can be valuable for many. Using illustrations and interactive tools could prove much more engaging than solely inviting feedback via a survey. Being considerate of the preferences of different ages and generations can also be useful. Sharing the strategy in a range of settings, with various groups, reinforces the collaborative nature of the whole process, bringing much-needed clarity and purpose for everyone.

5   *Implementation* – put the plan into practice. After what may have been a lengthy planning and research process, momentum can sometimes be lost once the time to implement the plan arrives. Yet this is the exciting point when ideas and possibilities can finally be put into action and we can catch a glimpse of all that God has in store for our families. As the strategy evolves and takes shape, these first steps move our dreams for ministry with families into meaningful and invigorating reality. Depending on the nature of the plan and the timescale, it can be invaluable to include others and take a team approach with members willing to push forward with specific aspects, using their expertise and skills more effectively. This will enable us to discuss and adjust if necessary, building in some flexibility as the strategy unfolds. And flexibility, not sticking dogmatically to every last detail, will prove beneficial, especially if we encounter hurdles or unforeseen setbacks.

6   *Review* – take stock. Once the strategic plan has had time to become embedded in the life of the church, we need to ensure that we dedicate time to reviewing how the process has developed in practice. Ask honest questions about how it's making an impact, where there are signs of effectiveness and who with. In essence, discover if it's making a difference and addressing the goals we originally set. It may be that aspects of the plan need amending; we may need to alter our approach

in some way. Having these discussions with others, especially with the families in our context, will help us do this well.

As family ministry practitioners, developing this reflective attitude to what we do can be highly constructive. Maintaining an awareness of how our overall aims are being met and how we're utilising resources to do this, and considering alternative routes if necessary, can ensure that our strategy remains relevant. We may not naturally incline towards this kind of reflection, and we may need one or two others to help us, but our ministry will benefit from it as we're able to bring our enhanced perspective to bear on the future development of our work with families.

These six stages take us from musing over what might be to seeing the fruit of our labour thrive and grow around us. At each step we have an opportunity to consider the direction we're moving in and how best to minister effectively to those in our churches and communities.

It should go without saying that to embark on a strategic process such as this needs to still be a spiritual and faith-deepening activity. As we trust in God, in his plans for us as his people, we strive to walk step by step into all he has in store for us. Our priorities and strategy are developed in light of all we know him to be and of our desire to make him known in the world. If we ensure that God remains intrinsic to the process of identifying the way forward for our family ministry, we can be assured that he lives and breathes through and into it.

Conclusion

Being willing to undertake the type of lengthy process we have been discussing may be unappealing when we're keen to just get on and do the work of family ministry. If we're relational people, planning and priority setting may seem tedious in comparison to spending time with parents and children. But being strategic when embarking on family ministry can prove transformational, both for our practice and for the families we know, support and live with. And ensuring there is scope to reflect and review once our strategy is implemented will allow it to continue developing and making an impact.

Garland's four principles provide a foundation for developing our strategic thinking in family ministry. She argues that opportunities to strengthen and disciple families, to help them grow in both relationship and faith with one another, should be woven into the formal and informal times when we gather as a whole church, rather than creating new programmes or groups to serve these purposes that stand separate from existing ministry forums.

This helpful approach sees congregational life as a means to develop further routes into family ministry practice, integrating it with the times and places where families are already gathering. It's not necessarily about starting from scratch, taking a blank sheet to map out a pristine new ministry plan, but instead identifying where we can build on those things God is already giving light and life to. This can prevent church life from becoming dense and over-programmed, so that families struggle to prioritise where and when to participate. By striving to streamline and offer well-defined occasions when family ministry takes place, we can shape practice that is sustainable, utilising our time and money more effectively.

By adopting a plan for our ministry, we can avoid the danger of jumping in too quickly before having a clear sense of what the goals are or how these might be accomplished. In carefully considering what is genuinely required, we can make better use of our resources and energy. We won't instantly feel inclined to seize a new programme, hoping it will address all the areas we're aware of; instead we can assess at a later point if such a programme is a good route to follow once we've done our research and consulted with the families in our churches and communities. By discovering what matters to the families and how we can work together to enhance their lived experience, we place families at the core of our work and practice, recognising the significance of their engagement that influences the shape of what we do. By being strategic, our watchword can be 'simplicity', keeping our family ministry true to our principles and not inadvertently creating a complex web of activity that drains life and punishes us in the process as practitioners.

From a strategic perspective this type of ministry with families is holistic, the enterprise of the whole church: practitioners, clergy, leadership teams and congregations joining together to mutually support all different kinds of families, providing opportunities for them to build relationships with one another and learn from each other. In this context the practitioner is a facilitator, investing his or her energy in providing the setting where this rich and multifaceted environment is cultivated for all, individually and corporately. In essence, being strategic liberates us, as it releases greater opportunities to observe the profound and mysterious work of God happening in and around us – in the lives of parents, children, grandparents and all those we call kin in our households, clans, neighbourhoods and the body of Christ, the church.

Questions for reflection

- What principles underpin your work and practice with families?

- How do the 'four dangers' ring true for you in your experience?

- What could be the barriers to your adopting a strategic approach in the work you do?

- What could be the starting point for your research?

- Who might you want to involve in developing a strategic plan for family ministry in your context?

- Do you consider yourself a reflective practitioner? What could help you develop in this area?

5

BE SUPPORTIVE

Introduction

My time serving as a family pastor drove home to me the central role of the local church in supporting families. Whether informal (chats with parents and carers as they arrived at the toddler group) or formal (courses on parenting skills), so much of what our church did was designed intentionally to strengthen families, especially in the early years of a child's life. But pinpointing exactly what we meant by 'support' wasn't straightforward. It was difficult to capture its essence, but for us it spoke of an approach to ministry that enhanced how families functioned.

Family support is a concept that continues to elude strict definition. For the purposes of this guide, however, I use 'support' to mean seeking to promote parenting confidence, increase self-esteem and nurture relationships between parents and children. It's deeply rooted in a longing to see families develop greater connectedness, enjoying a sense of well-being living with and alongside each other.

There are myriad ways to support families through the provision of activities, groups, courses and programmes. Some churches will choose a structured format; others a less formal one. There are, however, some widely acknowledged features as well as specific opportunities many churches will have in common. These can be excellent vehicles through which support networks can be nurtured and developed. We'll explore some of these practical routes into support later in the chapter. It may be that, instead of creating a new group or session from scratch, there are among the programmes we already offer opportunities to enhance provision further, amending current practice to incorporate new features.

Through toddler groups, coffee drop-ins, school holiday activities and seasonal celebrations, such as Christmas and Easter, our busy calendars may already have huge potential. Being alert to these possibilities is another dimension to maturing in our family ministry practice. Ensuring that we start by meeting families where they are, establishing dialogue and being excellent listeners will enable us to offer genuine support.

Features of support

One of my observations about ministry to families is how providing support is woven into the very fabric of so much of what we do. It's taken for granted that we're striving to be caring and boost a family's sense of well-being through their participation in the programmes and activities offered. Support is often a given, forming a core part of how we organise our ministry activities in church, but there are a number of factors to take into account when embarking upon this. These include: being family-centred, signposting other services, getting peer support, ensuring provision is accessible and being God-inspired. Let's unpack these one by one.

Family-centred

Being family-centred is the first strand in how we approach the kind of support we make available to families. It places the voices, views and thoughts of parents, carers and children at the core. Understanding a family's story – who they are, where they've come from, the issues they face – means we get a holistic picture of their life together. Rather than simply taking a snapshot, as we build relationships over time we gain a truer sense of a family's identity. As we've reflected previously, unless we have a clear understanding of what needs exist, it can easily be the case that our provision simply doesn't meet what families require.

By placing families in the centre, they become the drivers for the type of ministry activities we choose to pursue. It aids our decision-making in deciding to offer one type of group or session over another and aids us in prioritising where to begin. All the practical aspects of how support happens is guided by the kinds of families in our setting, from the times and places they occur in to whether food is included or a fee is charged (often one of the most challenging questions). Our families frame the responses to these as we reflect on how and when will suit them best.

Signposting

Secondly we accept that in church-based ministry it's impossible to meet every need a family may have. Our resources of time, money and energy and our pool of volunteers are finite. With the best will in the world, we simply can't do it all! Ensuring we can signpost families to other support is vital. We can inform them about the other places, venues, agencies and organisations where they may be able to access the provision that is right for them. This is especially true when families have specific needs or concerns or which specialist knowledge and understanding is required.

Signposting gives families further options they can either pursue themselves or we can accompany and facilitate their way into. It can often be useful to keep a core list of important websites or phone numbers for these local services that makes for easy reference to create a noticeboard where they're visible to all. As our church-based support develops, our list of contacts may grow too, so that signposting the most relevant and reliable services becomes less demanding. Putting the work into researching and seeking out what's available locally at the outset can pay off in the long run.

Peer support

In the early days of my ministry with families I now recognise some major flaws in how I approached my work and role. One of these was to assume that I needed to be the sole conduit for support. This may sound arrogant or ridiculous, but it is the misguided notion of many family ministry practitioners. I thought that I alone needed to provide families with the care and empathy they needed. In reality, no one person can ever deliver what everyone needs. As much as we might strive to befriend every family in our setting, we simply cannot meet all the demands presented. This might be a significant element that for some of us has the potential to transform the way we work out our family ministry practice.

Instead of striving to be the fount of all support, we need to adopt an approach that encourages families to mutually support each other. We are to be the facilitators that bring together parents, carers, children, teenagers, grandparents (or any combination therein): building friendships, sharing pressures and difficulties and joys, and offering advice to each other on ways to overcome these challenges. Often someone who has already walked that road can offer better counsel, simply because they've been there. Incorporating opportunities for peer support – parent to parent, carer to carer, grandparent to grandparent – can transform not only the lives of the families we work with but also the burden many practitioners carry as they endeavour to do it all.

Accessibility

Ensuring our provision is accessible should go without saying: today we're much more familiar with the term and recognise the need to consider how people can fully participate in church life and ministry. We should be going beyond the physical aspects this involves (such as accommodating those who are less mobile or vision impaired, for instance) to consider how the environment may hinder or help people's ability to get involved. Are there quiet spaces available? How easily can toys or resources be reached? Are there picture signs and labels as well as written ones? We may need to invite a fresh pair of eyes into our groups or settings to gain a better understanding of where the weak points are.

Whenever we take steps to reflect how accessible our provision is, we should recognise the importance of supporting the inclusion of everyone, perhaps through making modifications that improve access for those who have additional needs, but which often prove to be valued by our communities more widely. This happens not only through implementing support strategies (for example by using visual aids) but also through how we model inclusive practice when interacting with parents, carers and children. This encourages everyone to become more aware of how we welcome and engage with people of all different kinds in a range of ministry settings.

There is a wealth of resources available to aid practitioners here: the Additional Needs Alliance (**additionalneedsalliance.org.uk**) and Livability (**livability.org.uk**) are both good places to start.

God-inspired

Finally, we want to recognise the spiritual dimension of our support of families, the feature that makes church-based ministry distinct from other places where care may be accessed. Ministry with families is important because God loves families, and our support is God-inspired in how we relate to and treat people. If our hope is to reflect Jesus, then we'll want to engage with parents, carers and children with compassion and kindness, seeing them as neighbours loved overwhelmingly by our creator God. Extending this love to those we encounter in the flow of ministry marks us out as different, as followers of Jesus. Each encounter with a parent, carer or child, whether momentary or over the long term, leaves a trace of Christ in their lives. As we serve with no concern of receiving in return or expectation of our actions being rewarded, we have the promise of powerfully embodying the gospel. Our faith is working out through myriads of daily interactions which comprise the essence of our discipleship. Embracing God in the midst of what we do, seeking him in prayer, inviting him to dwell via the Holy Spirit in all our ministry activity brings provision to spiritual life, moving it from being simply a set of activities to a living expression of God with us.

How we bring this faith dimension overtly into our practice will vary from context to context, but it is vital that we are intentional about doing so. Providing opportunities for prayer, sharing the Christian story and scripture, celebrating the festivals and inviting everyone to participate can powerfully convey who we are as people of faith. It can be daunting to step out in this way – much of recent family work has sought to diminish explicit references to Christian faith and belief – but there are ways to do this well, in a manner that informs and encourages rather than indoctrinates. Often those participating in family ministry have a host of questions about God, faith and church, so providing spaces for these to be aired and responded to can be refreshing. Finding the means to do this in a way that is relevant and meaningful for families in your setting is the key, so giving something a try and taking a chance to open up conversations is always better than ignoring the spiritual dimension in what we do. Have courage.

Making support relevant

Our next step is to identify the opportunities for supporting families. This entails considering three factors. Spending time assessing these in advance aids us in determining how appropriate a particular activity might be. It also means support is tailored effectively to those participating, making it fit for purpose.

Formal or informal

The first question is whether to offer something formal or informal. If our intention is to nurture education, we may want to pursue a more formal structure, such as running a parenting course. If we're looking to encourage greater friendship and mutual support, we may feel that something informal is more suitable.

In the 21st century, many parents reject the school-like environment of multi-session courses, finding them to be too rigid and goal-oriented, where the assumption is that there is a 'correct' way to parent and that if they adopt all the principles shared they will be much better parents. It's a very direct and one-way approach that assumes parents are unskilled and have no insight to offer. For many, to attend a course implies that they've somehow fallen short, aren't good enough and are getting the whole parenting job wrong; they will run a mile rather than be criticised for how they're raising their children.

Overcoming these presumptions is a challenge. Reassuring parents and carers that a formal course of learning can enhance their parenting skills isn't always easy. Often it boils down to the degree of relationship a practitioner has with a family and the level of trust that exists between them. There are also other barriers to parents and carers signing up for courses, such as childcare and time, so exploring ways to reduce these barriers is important if we plan to establish contexts for more formal learning. Finding settings other than a church building (which can symbolise authority and institution), such as a family home or coffee shop, can be helpful. The right venue will depend on who the audience for the learning is and where they prefer to congregate. It's more often the case that formal learning opportunities can be woven into informal occasions, maybe in bite-sized chunks, which nurture dialogue and reflection with a group so there's space to discuss and apply to everyday life. Combining this with a time for families, parents and carers to eat together can be beneficial for everyone, as it boosts their well-being and is easier to integrate into hectic lifestyles.

Shared interests and need

The second question to consider is whether support can be generated around shared interests and need. This can be another fruitful route into gathering people. There's likely to be a higher chance that parents and carers (and their children, potentially) will participate if what they're engaged in is fun and enjoyable, a good use of their leisure time and felt to be rewarding. Learning about what kind of interests there are and where, who with and when they take place will help us to match support activities well with those taking part. If the support generates an improved sense of well-being for the whole family, builds confidence for those in parenting roles and offers much-needed breathing space for laughter and enjoyment, it has to be a good thing! The benefits of joining in are multiplied when the activity clearly delivers on a number of different levels. So whether it's walking in the woods, being creative through craft, a bike ride, gathering round a bonfire, cooking a meal from scratch, watching a football match, working together on a street clear-up or sitting down to enjoy a movie, there are endless ways we can provide a setting where families can experience support as well as being caring to others joining in.

Different ages

Finally, we need to consider how age-appropriate the support being provided is. Is it taking place at the right time for those with young families? If teens are involved, what's going to work best for them? How long an activity will last is also dependent on the ages of those joining in. Think about how much sitting and listening is involved – not simply for the children; many adults are not keen to remain still, preferring more active routes to explore and grow their knowledge and understanding.

Being aware of the ages and stages of those participating will impact on our environment-related choices, such as the layout of a room, the music played, the furniture and the resources offered. Our choice of language will also be key: if parents and children are together, we will perhaps want to strike a tone different from a meeting of parents only. Being aware of the need to include children and young people, addressing questions to them and encouraging them to lead or join in with activities can encourage fuller intergenerational participation beyond solely adult-to-adult conversation. Creativity can be the key here in providing a range of different ways to share thoughts and ideas that raise everyone's ability to join in meaningfully. Our various styles of learning and participation are obviously not dependent on our age in years, yet remain important to reflect on when exploring the format provision takes.

Once we've established the format for support, bearing in mind these features and how to ensure its relevance, we're in a strong position to begin the process of inviting and encouraging families to get involved. It's much more likely that the impact of provision will be multiplied if we spend time in advance getting these aspects right – matching support to people, placing families firmly at the centre, empowering them in the process. It's practitioner time very well spent.

Routes into support

The key next step in practice is to pinpoint when and where we can offer support to and build relationships with families. Many of these suggestions may already have been identified in the course of exploring your current family ministry practice, but it may be worth considering ways to extend or develop what's on offer. So let's wind a path through the various ages and stages of family life, recognising how provision can be tailored to parents, carers and children in those specific seasons.

Young families

The arrival of a newborn often causes huge upheaval in family life, particularly for first-time parents. This is wonderful, as the tiny new human being is welcomed into the world, but it also may mean that nothing will be the same again. Every new parent's experience is different, but it's undeniable that becoming a family with young children changes the course of everyday life, as well as the relationship between those caring for them. It's a significant and obvious time to offer support. Make contact by sending a welcome card and gift, sharing details of local services such as baby clinics, or ask if others in the church family can pitch in and help by cooking meals, doing some laundry or popping in to babysit, so exhausted parents can sleep. It's good to have a response in place so that when a baby arrives there's an easy process to follow. I learnt early on when we launched a group for new parents that many of them valued the chance to chat and share about all the new, often alien, experiences they found themselves having. But also, for many of them it was a rare treat just to be able to enjoy a cup of tea while someone else held their newborn – the group offered a degree of respite which was so important to those fledgling parents.

Toddler groups are a logical next step as a supportive environment, and indeed many churches around the country already run these kinds of groups. The usual format includes laying out various toys, leading a time of singing or storytelling, offering a craft activity and having a break for a drink and snack. (The 'hot drink dilemma' continues in many settings, with the best way to offer tea and coffee an ongoing debate!) In settings where toddler groups have existed for many years a regular review – both of format and function – can be useful. Checking whether toys, games, furniture and resources need replacing (they often do) is advisable. It's well worth considering whether to change the format (such as having story time instead of a singing session, or rotating the toys so not everything is available at every session), especially if the group involves volunteers. Toddler groups can be superb environments to nurture peer support and to draw regular attendees into helping set up and organise the running of the group; they often become little communities where strong friendships are formed. Both the Early Years Alliance and Playtime (from Care for the Family) offer a wealth of resources for toddler groups, from practical guidance and policies to top tips and creative ideas.

For some parents, the arrival of a child, with all the wonder, joy and extra responsibility he or she brings, triggers an abundance of questions about life, purpose and what it means to parent. The opportunities to explore such spiritual questions, to ponder on meaning and to muse on why we're here can be significant, and the church is ideally placed to help parents unpack their big questions about life. In this season of life, some families may be curious to learn more about christening or baptising their child. For those without church or faith backgrounds, these may be unfamiliar rites of passage that require explanation of what's involved. Denominations have various resources outlining this ritual that can be useful as 'takeaways' for parents to refer to at a later date. Be open and informative with young families about what being christened or baptised means. Parents often warmly receive this opportunity to celebrate the life of their child. Finding ways for the church to be actively involved in these precious years is sometimes dismissed as simply being a one-off, yet it can lay the foundations for the coming years when a family knows from experience that the church is a place of welcome, support and hopefulness. Why would we want to pass up an opportunity like that?

The primary years

As children grow and enter nursery and then school, family life enters a new era. With the physical, emotional and mental demands of raising children of this age, the primary years are a roller coaster of discovery, fun and mayhem along with exhaustion and downright hard work! Support during this season of life can include developing parents' skills, growing their confidence and sharing strategies that smooth the day-to-day running of households with younger children. Giving parents the space to get some much-needed time out, peace and adult conversation is a good place to start. Working with parents to grasp what they need, exploring whether a course could be the answer or looking at more informal opportunities, will determine how effective this is.

Families savour the time they get to spend together, which can be in short supply in busy households. Joining in at a local Messy Church is a simple and enjoyable way to learn, celebrate, explore faith and relax with other families, people of different ages, backgrounds and stages. Back when I was part of the team for our Messy Church it was always a joy seeing parents, carers, grandparents and children arrive after the busyness of the day and then relax into a couple of hours of easy time together. As we sat down to eat, amid the noise, chatter and mouth-watering smells, it was a pleasure to observe around the room the smiles and simple pleasure of eating with one another. Yes, it required dedication and hard graft to make happen (a definite gift of my colleague Jo!), but it powerfully and cheerfully gave families a space they treasured. I loved seeing a dad arrive once just after 5 o'clock, after leaving work. As dinner was served, he came in and sat down with his partner and kids, and listened to them tell him about school, the story they'd heard a moment ago and the songs they'd sung and then ask him if there was any ketchup. These moments of family life are precious indeed.

There's an abundance of resources available to help practitioners and workers plan and lead a Messy Church – a space for learning and worship that exists as church in its own right, not as an avenue into what some see as 'proper church' on a Sunday morning. These congregations need resource and investment – both in terms of our time and energy – many of which become firmly rooted communities in their local setting.

The teenage years

As children enter adolescence, support for families can be harder to come by. Whereas in a child's primary years, the school gate is often the place to share parenting ups and downs, once they head off to secondary school that network is not available in the same way. At work today, a colleague and I chatted about our teenage children. Afterwards, both of us reflected how helpful it had been to have a moment to share our current experiences raising teenagers – their requests for cash (we only want to pay for the essentials now), new part-time jobs and juggling social lives and schoolwork. Those 20 minutes ended up being time very well spent as we recognised the similar positions we found ourselves in.

For many parents it can be difficult to identify where to access support during what can often be turbulent years. Even as parents delight in seeing their offspring become more independent and launch into adult life, they can struggle to adapt to these new 'almost adults' in their midst. Church can be an ideal space to create opportunities for parents and teens to thrive, and not just survive, during this time. The teenage years involve some key stages, such as choosing options for GCSEs, approaching exams and considering the next steps of life and education, that can be valuable times to provide care, information and safe spaces for conversation and prayer.

Being alert to the needs of young people includes provision for mental health, which continues to be a significant issue and one the church is beginning to grasp. Knowing where local services for mental health can be found, growing our own understanding of it and developing routes for healthy conversations on the topic with young people may all be part of a family ministry strategy. Recognising the needs of parents and carers in this is hugely important too.

It may seem strange to include aspects of work with young people, as family ministry has predominantly been focused on younger families, but there's a strong case to be made that it's an overlooked area which is urgently in need of time, energy and focus. Parents with teenage children can feel they have few places to turn to in times of difficulty besides their child's school. Creating other support options, on neutral territory, such as church, could have the potential to improve the well-being of the whole family.

Families with adult children and empty nesters

Once children are grown up, in employment or further education, and no longer living at home, we might assume that our job in terms of ministry with families is done – that empty nesters are no longer part of our remit for ministry. Yet there's much to suggest that this is an often-neglected era in family life, when significant change happens, particularly for parents. Helping to prepare people for the next steps in their life together can prove enormously beneficial for their well-being. It can ensure their offspring are able to fly the nest, gain independence and flourish into adulthood with healthy levels of support and care.

Those with adult children can often be a valued resource in wider work with families, offering experience, a listening ear and encouragement to others in the earlier stages of raising children. Having been there themselves, they can be the ideal people to offer support and advice to parents going through challenges or struggling to know how to manage a specific set of circumstances. This kind of support may take the form of more informal care – conversations over coffee – or be established on a more formal basis, such as regular mentoring. Finding opportunities for them to do this in turn enables them to continue feeling connected to the church and community. People at this stage of life can be a prized treasure waiting to be discovered and involved in ministry. I've known many over the years who became stalwarts in ministry, graciously and faithfully investing in the lives of younger families, identifying ways to contribute that were mutually rewarding.

Grandparenting

The role of grandparents has evolved in recent decades from occupying a more honoured, less engaged role to being frequently involved with the day-to-day lives of their children and grandchildren. This shift from a passive to an active position has brought both pleasures and demands. Many grandparents are now the primary care providers, looking after infants and toddlers when parents return to work as well as seemingly running their own after-school clubs to care for their primary-age grandchildren once the school day has ended. I've lost count of how many family work practitioners have described the rise of grandparents in settings such as toddler groups. It's a new dynamic we should be aware of, as it impacts on how groups can function and relate to one another. In terms of raising involvement across generations this can be a very healthy development, welcoming a wealth of understanding and experience that can be shared and gleaned from.

The increased responsibilities have been a blessing for many, who enjoy this additional time seeing their grandchildren grow and develop, yet the accompanying challenges can be great. Resolving differences in parenting styles, establishing healthy boundaries and maintaining a life of their own can be hard to juggle. How can grandparents be supported as they navigate their way through all the complexities that this new phase brings? What are the best places to gather and facilitate support with others in a similar position?

As well as offering support to their own families, grandparents today are in need more than ever of their own spaces to receive care. Learning more about how this can be provided and made available would be welcomed by many in this season of life.

Hang on, what about single people?

It was reflected on occasion that it was a shame single people didn't get a mention in the *We Are Family* research report. The project presented a snapshot of what was currently taking place in family ministry, indicating that for many practitioners single people simply didn't appear in the work they found themselves doing. It raises interesting questions around who the audience for family ministry is and what place single people might have that could benefit both them and other families (besides being the obvious babysitters). Pioneering inclusive ways for everyone to participate could be on the horizon for us.

Conclusion

Our support strategies are multidimensional, and we've explored a range of ways it could be offered to families at different stages. There's a trend towards less structured and more informal approaches that can be more easily interwoven into the ebb and flow of family life. Families can be resistant or suspicious of opportunities that appear contrived or that contain faith-based elements they weren't expecting. Explaining from the outset what an event or get-together involves and roughly what happens can encourage people to join in and prevent awkward conversations later with those who felt misled by what they walked into. This is by no means a red flag about mentioning anything faith-related; I am simply urging transparency. In my own experience, offers to pray with or for others, to share personal testimony and to join in a celebration at Easter or Christmas were rarely dismissed because of their Christian roots. How we do more not less of this across our host of family-related activities is the real question – being creative, genuine and ready in our sharing of the gospel at all times.

Remember that the impact of support is felt over time. It's important, therefore, to review whether what's being offered is meeting a need. Taking an 'appreciative inquiry' approach, which proposes some key questions, could be a helpful tool to explore this. Purely crunching the numbers is not recommended; don't let statistics always be the judge of how well ministry is growing or making a difference. Inviting the views and reflections of those who participate could inform and shape development for the future much more purposefully.

Finally, for support to be welcome, useful and life-enhancing, we need to be prayerful, building trust and relationships with all family members we know and work with. Our role is to shape a ministry that's accessible and inclusive, recognising we all need support in a host of different ways at different times in life. We might find ourselves being providers and facilitators now, never knowing when that era of life descends when we're in need of care and compassion ourselves. Bearing this reciprocity in mind aids us in being empathetic practitioners, keen to recognise our mutual humanity and striving to extend kindness, even when it might be one of the hardest things for us personally to do.

Questions for reflection

- Explore what the word 'support' means for you. What connotations does it bring to mind?

- Is there a place or forum for support that no longer seems to be effective? Does it need to stop or be refreshed?

- Is there a particular group or stage of family life that isn't currently being supported? What might meet their need? Who else (individuals or organisations) might be able to help you do this?

6

BE COLLABORATIVE

Introduction

When I embarked on my teacher training in the late 1980s, it was obvious from the start that this wasn't a profession for those keen on lone working. Within those first few weeks we found ourselves in primary schools teaching in small groups and pairs, planning with others, leading activities in the classroom together, and reflecting and evaluating our practice with each other afterwards. Even in those early, stumbling days of our training, teaching was very much understood to be a team effort. We couldn't do it without the input and support of our colleagues.

Since then, this team ethos has become embedded in my approach to all aspects of work and ministry. It's simply an instinct. It has underpinned everything I do in church with a recognition that we are able to accomplish more, create more sustainable work and develop personally as we intentionally collaborate and invite others to join us in the privilege of ministry life. If I'd resolved to be a one-woman band I'm certain we'd never have progressed very far: new ideas would never have been tried, ambitious projects would never have got off the ground and vital learning would never have been received. Only through actively choosing to engage with others has it often been possible to achieve those exciting goals and move things forward.

We can't do ministry alone. We need the diverse voices, ideas and input of others in order to offer families the best support and enable them to access all the church has to offer. We can, of course, try, but the fruit of our labour will be short-lived and often end with demoralisation and exhaustion. It is essential that we find ways to collaborate, employ the gifts and talents of others and release them so that they can fulfil all their God-given potential. We're in this together.

Understanding the opportunities and ways to collaborate is important in how we approach ministry with families. From building relationships with parents, children and their wider family, through gathering volunteers and linking with other staff, to identifying and establishing partnerships with other churches and organisations – all these actions have at their core a desire to shape ministry together. Doing this well and being intentional in seeking out the right people or places depending on the task is key.

For anyone setting out in a new role, getting to know those in our context and locality is enormously important. As we explored in chapter 4, building our knowledge and understanding of where we're based can make a huge difference and embed ministry firmly in the lives of the people who find themselves there. If our work is to be authentic and meaningful, this is our route to making a difference. In this chapter we'll explore the three core participants and partners for family ministry: the families themselves, our church colleagues and the agencies that exist beyond our immediate work vicinity. Throughout keep your own setting in mind, identifying whom this may mean you're being called to collaborate or partner with, all the while recognising the extraordinary mystery of how God works through us as we join others in the wonder of extending his kingdom.

Working together with families

At the core of family ministry is relationship-building with families. It establishes trust, helps us understand how groups of individuals function as families and reveals the types of challenges families face, enabling us to tailor what we do to best meet the needs of those around us. Family work in all its forms has this as a key task. It is foundational for any support that's offered.

What that relationship-building looks like in practice continues to be debated, even outside church contexts, such as in education and social work: it's 'both a style of work and a set of activities that reinforce positive informal social networks through integrated programmes'.[69] The word 'informal' here is helpful, as it highlights how much interaction occurs in natural, everyday surroundings – simple conversations that take place in meetings, over coffee or during a chance encounter at the shops or in the street. As Diana Garland writes, 'Wherever possible, it is better to lean toward the informal, the participatory and the relational rather than the formal, the performance and the outcome focused.'[70] These are the ways relationship steadily grows and support is extended.

It is unwise to assume that we know what families need and not bother to ask them. Garland differentiates between 'ascribed' and 'felt' needs: those that practitioners and leaders identify, whether a family experiences them or not, and those that families themselves believe they have. It's an important distinction. We may only see, in our communities and the families whom we interact with, what we anticipate seeing. Our own assumptions, experience and perspective mean it's almost impossible to take an objective view. It may not be the full picture of who each family is. The struggles of putting toddlers to bed, late-night disagreements with teenagers, juggling work and childcare, caring for a parent with dementia, keeping good lines of communication open with ex-partners, getting support for children with additional needs – all these may be occurring behind closed doors, and finding out who a family is takes time and dedication. As Emma Sawyer and Sheryl Burton say (in the context of early intervention), 'Generalisations and value judgements need to be guarded against.'[71] As far as possible, being alert to our biases and viewing each family as a unique entity will protect against this.

In addition, occasionally families will hide who they really are, as Garland reminds us: 'Church is the last place they would let their troubles be known openly.'[72] Many of us can relate to the idea of being our 'best selves' when in a church service, a place where we'd be reluctant to acknowledge the messier stuff of our lives. Creating a culture where families feel able to be open is well worth pursuing. Some families may be poorly integrated into social groups for a number of reasons, not least if they're experiencing poverty, which can lead to isolation from others and from the possible support this could offer them. When families know that there are sound community resources on their doorstep, it minimises the impact of difficult circumstances and builds their resilience.

Families need times to voice their own concerns and views; such opportunities can be profoundly empowering. As practitioners, it is essential that we develop our ability to listen and ask open questions, and that we provide those moments for stories to be told and heard.

Family support in church often equates to pastoral care, the type of support that can occur through conversations over a cup of tea in someone's home. We mustn't underestimate the value of these times spent with parents, children and carers. Practitioners can occasionally feel that these discussions aren't the best use of their time, as they feel under pressure to account for their hours and working time. But it's often true that half an hour spent with a parent who feels under pressure can make a disproportionate difference to how that family continues to function at home, working through their current difficulties together. It's never time wasted but rather time well spent.

Consulting with the whole family can be a constructive way to generate a sense of partnership. Relationships tend to be built between adults, but family ministry demands that we take a wider view. Including children and young people, hearing their thoughts and views, can raise levels of participation and gives a more rounded sense of who a family is and how they operate. Conversely, neglecting to engage with the younger (or elderly) family members may give a distorted view, so it's useful to try to include everyone in the household as far as possible. If we believe family support to be a proactive process, recognising and encouraging all parties to fully participate can be invaluable and aid a family in gaining a fuller sense of well-being.

Deciding what kind of support to offer families can be difficult – whether to pursue a very structured approach (e.g. via a parenting course) or one that's more informal and tailored to a family's specific needs. Striving to build in a degree of flexibility can prove helpful, and continuing to be in dialogue with a family ensures that any provision is fit for the situation it's serving. At the heart of these approaches remains the principle of investing in the relationship. As practitioners we do well to remember:

Family support is about human interactions and people supporting other people, and a core condition for this to be successful lies within the strength, trust and sense of closeness, reciprocity and durability of the relationship between the caregiver and recipient. Within informal systems, trust is the glue of social capital.[73]

So the networks of relationships we choose to invest in and the people we intentionally spend time supporting will benefit from knowing they're built on that foundation of mutual trust. For a family to know there is someone locally who is reliable and interested in their well-being can have a huge impact. Encouraging these supportive social networks in and through the ministry we offer into our communities can build resilience in families, too, so they're better equipped to face the challenges and stresses of everyday life.

Viewing family ministry within the context of community recognises that support is offered on this premise to *strengthen* families, a key word that underpins what we do, starting where they are. As Garland writes:

- All families have strengths that are particular to their cultural background, beliefs and current situation.
- Families are doing the best they can, and their problems point to a lack of needed community resources and support.
- The best care of families focuses and builds on their strengths and resources rather than perceiving them as being 'broken' and needing to be 'fixed'.
- The goal of family services must be viewed 'not as "doing" for people but rather as strengthening the functioning of families'.[74]

Keeping this in mind when planning programmes and groups offers an invaluable perspective and aids us in approaching ministry activity in a way that is accessible and empowering for families.

It's useful to reflect on the boundaries that may need to be established here, giving consideration to the professional nature of those relationships. Working out the limits of how we may choose to interact and engage with people is important so that everyone has a shared understanding. By valuing the relationships we have with families and ensuring we continue to invest and support them, respect and trust can be built solidly over time. There are no shortcuts to getting to know families well besides determined commitment, week in and week out, which conveys clearly to them that they are seen, heard and welcomed.

Collaborating with colleagues

Being part of a church staff team is the next strand of how we adopt a collaborative approach to family ministry. Recognising that ministry is a joint enterprise that we engage in as a team needs to be embedded in our ethos. It's a key element of our ability to advocate for families and to ensure a voice is heard across the life of the church – recognising that family ministry needs to be woven through our experiences when we gather for worship and fellowship together. Keeping our colleagues informed of our work, seeking their support and guidance, and identifying opportunities to work together are all key elements of our teamwork.

There's an essential distinction to be made here in understanding our role as family ministry practitioners – we aren't necessarily the people called to do the work; instead, we are called to advocate for families. As Garland reminds us:

> Family ministry leaders, then, are not primarily the ones doing family ministry; instead they are the ones who remind, call to collaboration and orchestrate the leadership of others in the diversity of the church's activities and programs. In short, family ministry leaders are family advocates.[75]

Of course, in many instances it will be us doing the practical work of ministry, and we will bear the privilege of serving families in a host of different ways. But what should drive what we do is an understanding that our role is to campaign church-wide on behalf of families, striving to promote better outcomes for them. It may not always be easy, however, and we may have to help colleagues understand what ministry with families looks like, inviting them to actively participate in the diversity of what it is. Learning how we hold these dual elements of advocacy and practice is for us to work out as our experience grows and our identity as practitioners evolves.

Being a team player means being willing to share the ministry with colleagues, to develop strategy together, to plan in a way that offers cohesion to the activities of a church and to make those key decisions in consultation with them regarding what we will invest time and energy in and what we definitely won't. These conversations are vital if we are to pursue a sustainable model of ministry that is effective in the contexts we serve in.

Volunteers – those key people who can join us in the task of advocating for families – are also important to consider here. As we get to know others in our congregations, we can spot their strengths and provide opportunities for them to employ their gifts effectively. Two people stand out in my own experience – both in the context of an annual holiday club we were a team on. Friends Utd was an enormous enterprise to organise, growing from its early days of a few dozen children to over 100 a few years later.

Rachel stepped in to coordinate all the logistics and administration, ensuring registration ran smoothly and refreshments were available. I was all too aware this wasn't my area of strength, so knowing that her skills and abilities were being well utilised to run the club efficiently was hugely reassuring. She was dedicated to the task of getting the details right, and I admired her greatly for investing so much time and energy. The club ran all the better for her gifts being put to perfect use in this way.

Meanwhile I was able to work with Pip as we meandered through early theme ideas and discussions, dreamt up set designs, made programme plans and wrote teaching material. Our mutual creativity was harnessed to land upon fun and engaging ways to communicate with children and ensure they had a fantastic time during those week-long events. I have fond memories of working together and will forever have a debt of gratitude to her for all that she gave: her imagination, inventiveness and determination to hunt down resources and be wholeheartedly committed to forming memorable, faith-filled times for all those who joined us. She's one of a kind.

I feel very fortunate to have found such dedicated and wonderful people as Pip and Rachel. It can take time to discover who these people are, and we underappreciate them and their gifts at our peril. Identifying volunteers – those we can work alongside and invest deeply in – can bear great fruit if we pledge to make it a priority.

This connects with the ideas Robert C. Crosby presents when he discusses the idea of 'circles of teamwork', one that we see in action through the course of Jesus' ministry. Jesus knew perfectly how to draw people into the circles of his unfolding ministry, and he understood the nature of being engaged in the task of ministry with others: 'He built teams and communities in ways that people found absolutely compelling and frequently irresistible.' It was fundamental to how his work developed: a ministry that wasn't isolated but was actively drawing others in to live, work and serve. It demonstrates, argues Crosby, that God designed us for this very purpose: that we're not intended to embark on our own but instead to discover our own circles within which 'to dwell, live and thrive'.[76]

Beyond our church congregations we can explore becoming communities of practice with other practitioners in the vicinity. Where are there other practitioners engaged in the same work as us, and how might we go about building relationships with them so we better understand what they do and how they do it? How can we learn what family ministry looks like for them in their setting? Perhaps we might do this through attending conferences or training days together or simply gathering for lunch and reflecting on some recent reading. We can grow profoundly as practitioners through our willingness to commit to others, recognising we're all in the process of developing in our practice, knowledge and understanding.

Partnering with other organisations

I mentioned at the start of the chapter that from my first days of training it was obvious that teaching was very much a team enterprise. The same is true of supporting families. As a teacher, I was part of a wider network of support staff, advisers, governors, therapists and social workers who sought to create a framework of care. Some families required intensive ongoing support, whereas for others it was short-term intervention that made a difference. For all the shortcomings of our social care system (in terms of long waiting times for referrals or staff shortages) there was primarily a hope to improve outcomes for parents and children. In my experience churches have often been unaware of the wealth of resources on their doorstep that could be valuable to direct families towards.

During the course of the *We Are Family* research project we met many practitioners who had leveraged other provision, seeking local charities or organisations to broaden the reach of their family ministry. Much of what is termed 'family ministry' can also be considered community development, as we set out to meet the needs of those living in the church vicinity. Establishing contact with these community groups, facilities and agencies is important, as we can then identify specific opportunities where partnerships could be pursued. Whether getting to know the staff at the local schools, discovering that another church operates a food bank or finding out that a dementia support group meets monthly in the community hall, there are always places where linking up could be useful and appreciated by the families we encounter.

At the church in Luton where I was in lay ministry, there was a thriving programme for families with under 5s. We ran toddler groups four days a week, which were enormously popular, even attracting parents from the other side of town. Given the good reputation of these groups, it's perhaps not surprising that when the provision of a children's centre in the town was being discussed, the church was approached to become a hub. We sat around the table with two local primary schools, a preschool, two high schools, and the local surgery and health service, all of whom we knew well or had some form of contact with. During the course of our meetings those prior relationships bore fruit in forming a proposal around our church becoming a hub for universal provision, a base for child and parent support at the heart of our community. Indeed, there was significant agreement between all agencies to do this, which was extraordinary given it was a partnership of faith- and non-faith-based organisations.

Some of the invaluable lessons learnt from this experience included the need to identify those agencies who may offer specialist services that could be useful to our families, for instance, those provided by the local authority, by smaller charities and by other churches. Entering into partnership with other organisations requires a cooperative spirit and a willingness to explore where our common intentions lie and to compromise on occasion. This can be a point of dispute, if it's perceived that the compromise is faith-related; robust discussions on this topic are often necessary so that all parties have a clear notion of each other's identity.

Being a community-facing, community-supporting church requires us to be open to the possibilities God may be giving us. Through prayer and pursuit of him it can be rewarding not only for those directly involved, but also for the parents, carers and children in our neighbourhoods. It may take some courage on our part, but the rewards can be divine!

There are numerous organisations and resources available which may be operating or active in your neighbourhood. Here are some examples:

- Action for Children – a charity committed to helping vulnerable and neglected children and young people, and their families, via projects and services based around the UK. **actionforchildren.org.uk**

- Care for the Family – a national Christian charity that aims to promote strong family life and to help those who face family difficulties, through creating resources as well as running events and courses across the UK. **careforthefamily.org.uk**

- Children's Centre services – these continue to provide a range of services for early-years families in many locations. Find out more about what's on offer where you are by checking your local authority website. **gov.uk/ find-local-council**

- The Children's Society – a national charity that works with the country's most disadvantaged children and young people, in partnership with the Church of England, seeking to help them aspire to better lives. **childrenssociety.org.uk**

- Early Years Alliance – a charity which is the most representative early-years membership organisation in England. It supports them to deliver care, information and advice as well as campaigning to influence early-years policy and practice. **eyalliance.org.uk**

- Family Action – a charity seeking to build stronger families by providing practical, emotional and financial support to those who are experiencing poverty, disadvantage and social isolation across the country. **family-action.org.uk**

- Family Lives – a charity transforming the lives of families, supporting parents and helping them with any problems they face. It offers ongoing help on the phone, online or in local communities. It also informs, supports and trains professionals, campaigning for changes to improve family life. **familylives.org.uk**

- NSPCC – a national charity campaigning on child protection, seeking to prevent abuse, protect children and transform lives. **nspcc.org.uk**

It may well be worth exploring what provision these and other organisations offer in your area and how it may be possible to access their services. Churches Together exists in many places across the UK, and they may be able to direct you to further groups or activities operating locally.

Conclusion

Through the course of this chapter we've explored the principle of collaboration, which means understanding that ministry is best done in partnership. Whether that's with families themselves, colleagues and volunteers in our churches or those agencies and organisations in our locality, there's much to be gained from building our knowledge of these people and places. It can be easy to become consumed by the task of ministry, finding ourselves so caught up in the day-to-day service and care of others that it can become isolating. We can adopt an approach that's about 'doing to', with us as the primary 'solution finders' and others as the passive recipients of what we give, a model that allows us to maintain control rather than enter into potentially mutually rewarding and empowering partnerships. Recognising that we don't need to be (or rather that we should not be) lone, self-reliant ministry deliverers is liberating – it actively urges us towards finding fulfilling, rewarding partnerships with other people and organisations.

Bringing together the various interested parties – the families themselves, colleagues and external organisations – in the course of shaping our family ministry can be positive for all involved, not least us as practitioners. It can sink the roots of our church down into our local neighbourhoods and communities, so that it has a place much nearer the centre of the lives of residents. It encourages the church to be an inclusive place, accessible for anyone, knowing they can receive a welcome without any judgement attached.

Let's move away from a ministry approach that misleads us by assuming we can, and have to, do it all ourselves – a route that often leads to burnout. Instead, let's make an unswerving and bold commitment to an approach that recognises strength and significance in those we move and serve among. Let's embrace partnership and collaboration.

Questions for reflection

- Which families do you know whom it may be worth getting to know better?

- What kind of understanding do your colleagues have of family ministry? What type of steps could you take to make them better informed?

- What agencies or organisations are you aware of who are working in the local vicinity to your church? How much do you know about what they do or offer?

- Which agencies or organisations might it be worth contacting to support or extend the work that you're doing?

7

BE INTERGENERATIONAL

Introduction

The next habit that we can develop as we approach ministry with families is being intergenerational. Many of us will think that this is stating the obvious and be tempted to skip this chapter. Church is by its very nature a mixed-age community, where everyone, regardless of the generation they belong to, is part of the body of Christ. Scripture speaks plainly about making all welcome, so surely dedicating any thought to the topic isn't the best use of our time! But despite how obvious it may seem that there's a logical and unbreakable link between people of all ages and church life, it's an area in which we seem to have lost our way.

When we gather together as a church, so much time is spent with different ages in different spaces worshipping and learning in isolation. Our 'adult space' can often be seen as sacrosanct – we're reluctant to welcome children and young people into this space, because we're doing the hard work of faith as adults, dealing with the meaty issues and passages of scripture that they couldn't possibly handle. It's much simpler for them to be having fun, hanging out with their friends and hearing some of the basics of faith. Then there are the generational differences to overcome; each generation likes its own styles and formats, degrees of formality and traditions. So being separate makes a whole heap of sense, and it's just how it should be, right?

Whether we implicitly or explicitly hold those opinions, they reflect to a degree the current state of our attitudes in church when gathering as an intergenerational community. It's in a pretty sorry state. We've lost sight of how refreshing, rewarding and nurturing spending time together as different ages can be. Instead of trying to find ways to flourish as the whole church community, we've sought to sweep the issue under the carpet and hope it will go away, to each do our own thing as distinct generations. In this chapter, I argue that it's essential to revisit how we can thrive (and not just exist) together and I outline the benefits and bonuses of working hard to create relationships that span generations.

As a child my faith and sense of belonging was firmly forged through the life of the Methodist Church in north-east London, where I grew up. Being with people of different ages was an instinctive part of being church family. We worshipped together and often also spent time socially together. I have fond memories of the annual church picnic, heading off into Essex for food and fun, hanging out mainly with friends my age but interacting often with older people. I'm sure much of this was orchestrated and planned, but for me as a child and then a teenager, it felt very natural to be around people of different ages. Church was a place I was known by name, where I was encouraged to participate. Only later did I come to understand how vital it is to how we grow and belong as people of faith. Hearing older people pray, sing and value the Bible; leading alongside them; hearing words of encouragement from them; having them make time to be with me as I wrestled with life and things I didn't understand – all these aspects enabled and empowered me to know I belonged and was part of a thing called 'church', even if that wasn't fully grasped or understood. Being part of church community mattered to me, and I to it.

Church communities are one of the few places today where we find people of differing ages and generations. Yet much of the time we're separated by age group: children in crèches and Sunday school or children's church; our young people rarely engaging with anyone outside of their peer group. In recent times we've observed that so many of our congregations are ageing, asking why younger participants increasingly seem to disengage, go elsewhere or park their faith quietly while discovering adult life and its many challenges more widely. Something has happened that has disenfranchised them from feeling willing, able or enthusiastic about continuing to be the body of Christ wherever they find themselves. There is a whole heap of reasons, research and suggestions as to why this may be and how we can effectively respond (which many other books explore in more detail). At its core, though, lies the value of bringing the generations together – more often, more meaningfully and more relationally.

Children, young people and adults increasingly rarely meet in the course of church life; our programmes don't allow for it and we're often unsure how to do it well. So how can we rediscover our identity as 'one body', worshipping and growing authentic relationships that are beneficial for all? What ways of doing this might already be part of church life that with some tinkering could become places for deeper interaction? How can we overcome our hesitations and fears and treasure the joy and wonder of being genuinely intergenerational?

To start, we must assert that we need each other. From infants, toddlers, children and young people through to the retired, ageing and elderly – and everyone in between – there is so much to be gleaned and learnt from one another that can give a richness to our sense of our faith community together. Indeed why wouldn't we want to pursue greater contact across the generations? In this chapter we're going to explore some of the thinking around this as well as ways to develop as an intergenerational church where everyone flourishes. We need each other!

Have you ever given much thought to tying your shoelaces? What parts of the body are involved? Take a moment to think of the different body parts that are needed to do this simple task. How many did you come up with? Fingers, wrists, feet, ankles, knees for a start, as well as our spine, eyes, tendons, muscles and, of course, our brain to coordinate the whole sequence of different movements required. Such an everyday task requires a combination of different faculties and parts of the body. We can't simply put a pair of shoes on our feet and expect the laces to tie themselves; the rest of our body is needed to complete a relatively straightforward task.

There's a connection here to being an intergenerational community, and what this demonstrates is reflected in what we read in this passage from 1 Corinthians 12:

> The human body has many parts, but the many parts make up one whole body. So it is with the body of Christ… Yes, the body has many different parts, not just one part. If the foot says, 'I am not a part of the body because I am not a hand,' that does not make it any less a part of the body. And if the ear says, 'I am not part of the body because I am not an eye,' would that make it any less a part of the body? If the whole body were an eye, how would you hear? Or if your whole body were an ear, how would you smell anything? But our bodies have

many parts, and God has put each part just where he wants it… This makes for harmony among the members, so that all the members care for each other. If one part suffers, all the parts suffer with it, and if one part is honoured, all the parts are glad. All of you together are Christ's body, and each of you is a part of it.

1 CORINTHIANS 12:12, 14–18, 25–27

This passage reminds us that God designed the church to be a diverse body, consisting of a variety of people, backgrounds, ages and cultures – and that, in God's design, difference is good and lends strength and hope. From an intergenerational perspective, we need people of different ages as much as we need a variety of gifts and abilities to undertake the work of the church. The church is incomplete if it doesn't have a breadth of age groups – no generation is more valued or worthy than any other. Each has a mutual responsibility to the other to play its part, to contribute to the overall 'harmony' of the body as a whole. Building on this image of the church as a body, Eleanor Bird in her book *Blended* talks about the idea that when we strive to be an intergenerational community we become greater than the sum of our parts, that with God in the midst of us we're able to experience him more profoundly.[77]

When was the last time you spent time with someone from a different generation, that is, more than just to give a quick smile or say hello? Can you recall when you last had a conversation with someone elderly? Or a chat with a young adult where you found out something currently going on in their life? Or interacted with an excited toddler? You might be able to pinpoint many occasions, in which case that's excellent; but perhaps most of your recent conversations were with others in your peer group. We may have had these types of interactions in our own families at home, but I'd hazard a guess that for many these moments are much more scarce.

Over the past few weeks, I've spoken with my elderly neighbour, with my teenage and young-adult offspring, with friends of my own age and occasionally with their children. But this happens less and less; the older my friends' children get, the less time we spend in each other's company at shared get-togethers. It struck me at our last Christmas 'do' (when we invite our local friends and neighbours over) that few children now come, as they're all old enough to do their own thing. The time I spend with other generations is very limited, and that's probably not a very helpful thing!

At church, the opportunities for conversing with people in different generations appear to be very few. If I volunteer for children's work or Sunday school, I may get to know more of those under 11s, but on the whole I'm likely to find myself with people of a similar age or stage in life. My youngest child is in sixth form, and my eldest has just started his final year at university, so I'm on the brink of being an empty nester, and it's a huge help having others around in the same boat – both for support and also for those moments when I feel I need to let off a bit of steam! But spending time with other generations – speaking with them, building relationships with them – is very, very important. It grows empathy and understanding between us. It helps us have a sense of what struggles and challenges they face, the things that are on their mind. So how did we get here – where we've become a separated rather than an integrated body of believers?

One aspect that is easy to identify is how society and family life have changed exponentially since the childhoods of the senior members of our congregations. Extended families often lived close to each other – as I mentioned in chapter 1, in my own family my nan grew up in one house in her road, with her aunts and uncles and cousins living in the same street, only to get married and start her own family in the house next door. Everyone was connected, saw each other frequently and would be in and out of each other's homes regularly. They knew their relatives' business, how work was and the issues they were facing. Today, this is much rarer – families can often not be in the same country, let alone the same town or city. Generations don't mix or meet in the same everyday ways; it's more likely to be for a wedding, birthday or funeral or at Christmas. The notion of sharing life – living together or alongside – has a very different meaning for children and young people growing up today.

In church life, go back 100 years and families would often attend services together as part of the weekly rhythm of life. Children might go to an afternoon session of Sunday school, which was designed to educate and improve their basic skills in reading and writing. Later in the 20th century, Sunday school became incorporated into the morning worship of many congregations, and we still see in many places whole congregations worshipping together at the start of a service and then separating into discrete age groups.

During this time, there has also been an increased professionalisation of our work with children and young people. Workers are employed and bring skills that result in the church becoming the primary place where understanding of the faith grows. Bible curriculums have been written, and we've outsourced discipleship to the church to do as 'their job'. This, of course, reflects wider developments in family life – many children and young people go to 'the experts' for lessons in dance, sport, music and so on to improve their skills and abilities, but rarely are these occasions a whole-family experience. It's a peer one.

We also live in a postmodern world that values individualism. Western culture prioritises the needs of the individual and the owning of personal faith as opposed to a shared collective one. In this environment, we experience and grow in faith on a more isolated basis, where our questions are for our own contemplation and not for discussion among others. Much of contemporary life leads us, explicitly or otherwise, to developing a solitary life, and this undoubtedly impacts on our desire and ability to engage with others.

And this is all against a backdrop of decline in church involvement among children and young people. Steven Emery-Wright and Ed Mackenzie cite the example of Emily, describing her experience of Glastonbury, the hugely popular UK music festival, in comparison to church: 'I can't imagine anything happening in the church that could be relevant to my life.'[78] This is a sentiment no doubt shared by many others in her peer group. Recent research by the Church of England also highlights how fewer young people are participating in the church, a trend witnessed across all denominations, as they no longer perceive the church as being a relevant place to experience community.

Intergenerational church today

With authentic intergenerational community rarely our experience in the 21st century, we're left with a lot of questions. Family and children's workers often sense that something needs to change, but can't quite put their finger on exactly what that is – just that something has been lost along the way. As Peter N. Stearns writes, 'There are less regular and structured interactions between young and old... than ever before. Not only families but also other institutions in modern society have reduced the chance for old and young to share activities in meaningful ways.'[79] Perhaps we have been separating our church communities for too long or too effectively. Perhaps those in their 20s and 30s have opted out of church because they have been unable to find their place in it alongside other generations. Perhaps separating everyone for so long has made it virtually impossible to nurture whole-church communities, where the youngest through to the oldest are known to each other and can call each other by name. It's been said that western culture 'ghettoizes within generational borders'.

Separating out the different generations was an excellent strategy for a certain period. But now we need to go back and reflect on what it means to be an age-integrated or intergenerational community. We need to move beyond being a *multigenerational* church to becoming genuinely *intergenerational*. Sometimes these two terms are used interchangeably, but I think there's an important difference. Matthew DePrez defines them as like the shuffle button versus the repeat button on a music app.

Intergenerational ministry is like the shuffle button. There's an intersecting of the generations. They're not merely in the same room; they've walked across the room to talk to each other. They know about each other. They're deeply invested in each other's life. Intergenerational ministry is when a senior citizen calls a college freshman to let them know they're loved and missed. Or when a crisis happens in a high-school student's life, and they know they can count on an adult to listen.

Multigenerational ministry is like the repeat button. There's no intersecting of generations. They're all in the same room, but each generation is avoiding each other, intentionally or not. They're walking around the room but not across the room. Multigenerational ministry happens when children and students are sitting in the same Sunday morning service as the adults, but neither of the generations are talking to each other. Nobody knows more about the other generation than when they started the service. It's when they don't know about each other's passions and hobbies or their separate struggles, hurts and pains.

If we imagine these two images of the generations in the room as two ends of a spectrum, where would we place our own worshipping community? Would it be closer to the 'inter' or 'multi' generational end? Are we taking steps towards becoming more intergenerational and away from being merely multigenerational? It may well be worth pursuing this conversation with others in your context and exploring the idea in more depth. There is a difference here we need to grasp, as Peter Menconi says: 'An intergenerational philosophy differs from a multigenerational philosophy by intentionally involving as many generations as possible in the life and activities of the church.'[80] It's this bringing together of different generations that we want to invest time and energy in, recognising there are enormous benefits for everyone if we do.

Benefits of intergenerational community

The first benefit of nurturing an intergenerational church community is that it enhances and grows the faith of everyone. Not only does our own experience of God develop but also our discipleship as we walk alongside others – something that's been described as an ecology of faith nurture, as John Roberto says:

> Christian commitment is formed and strengthened as persons develop relationships and actively participate in a community that teaches, models and lives out the community's beliefs. People learn the ways of the community as they participate authentically and relationally with the more experienced members of the community.[81]

There is much to be gained from spending time with others whose faith may be new or more deeply established in terms of how we grasp what it means to be a believer. Being woven into the life of an intergenerational community provides the ideal setting: 'a primary network that helps faith grow,'[82] where we are able to worship and meet with God, growing in our understanding of the language of faith and the rites and rituals that are the markers for how it is lived out on a daily basis. For younger generations especially, the impact can be powerful: 'Weaving a thick web of such relationships can help young people not just to survive in their faith but flourish.'[83]

As we live and move with others of different generations, we're able to observe and experience the daily practice of what it means to be a follower of Christ. What we see in public can have a transformative effect on how we develop as disciples in private. For older generations and grandparents the notion of being a 'spiritual mentor' can offer a key role that both nurtures the faith of those younger and gives an opportunity to reflect on their own beliefs and experiences.

For Holly Catterton Allen and Christine Lawton Ross, faith maturity is fostered in environments where churches intentionally integrate various generations for 50–80% of congregational activities. Their extensive research points to the powerful impact of different ages in terms of faith development. In intergenerational settings faith is much more likely to thrive.[84]

A second benefit of being an intergenerational community is that we reflect the principle that everyone matters to God. It recognises that God created us equal, each with unique potential to contribute and shape our faith communities, regardless of our age, background or experience. When we gather intergenerationally we can share personal stories and explore faith issues from a whole range of circumstances. These build relationships and a sense of mutual understanding, as well as what Joseph Rhea describes as 'wisdom, wonder and godliness'.[85] Different ages reflect different understandings of who God is and how we each fulfil our purpose when in relationship with him. Referring back to the image of the body from 1 Corinthians 12, we see the real fruit of being the committed body of Christ, where people of all ages have the opportunity to offer and receive genuine care, support and love that grows beyond generational lines.

A third benefit of being a community that places a high value on all genera-tions is that it nurtures unity and a sense of belonging to 'the whole', counter to so much of modern living that is experienced as individuals. Menconi stresses that this must go beyond tolerating one another, moving towards a place where 'all members of the church must learn to genuinely appreciate people in the body who are different than themselves'.[86] In other words, we need to build sound relationships across the barriers that hinder us.

We also need to work towards a more equitable environment where power and authority can be shared by people of different ages. According to Martyn Payne, whose vast experience of Messy Church makes him a significant voice in this field, issues of equality are important when considering our intergenerational approaches; that is, no generation has authority over another, and both young and old have much to offer and to receive from each other.[87] Intergenerationality can be misconstrued as the flow of help in just one direction, 'downwards' from older to younger, but there is often much to be gained spiritually, practically and relationally from all generations mixing and building deeper relationships with others of differing ages.

We will then be able to come together, giving a perspective on life as we transition through the multiple stages we often experience in families – embarking on adulthood, having children, relationship difficulties, entering middle age, ageing parents, bereavement and so many other events that we share in common with others. An intergenerational community can be a vital support as we transition through the various seasons of life – to share our experiences with others who have already been there or to encourage those approaching them.

Moving towards intergenerational church life

Taking steps towards being more intergenerational (because, let's be honest, it's not something that will happen overnight) may seem daunting, but it is essential. In the context of family ministry, we need to consider not only the kinds of families we meet and what they need, but also the ages of those in our churches and communities and how best they can be brought together for mutual benefit.

Recently more grandparents have been participating in family ministry groups and activities, as, with more parents working full-time, they occupy new roles as childminders and caregivers. Rather than their retirement being a period of slowing down and rest, many grandparents find themselves in toddler groups and on the school run. Growing our understanding of the needs of grandparents today is important if our family ministry is to provide the kind of support that will make a difference to them.

If we want to explore becoming a more intergenerational community, there are three places you could choose to start from.

1 Gathering together

Pause and reflect on when the generations gather, identifying opportunities in church life and events. When and where are different generations together in the same room? Then consider how these times can be adapted to make them more meaningful – to nurture understanding and empathy and to generate a sense of being one body. This is not necessarily about creating additional programmes, spending huge amounts of time planning or completely overhauling our calendars or formats; it may be about working with the natural ebb and flow of how the church meets and simply enhancing the opportunities church life already presents, such as by building in moments to chat and get to know each other. 'To experience authentic Christian community and reap the huge blessings of intergenerationality, the generations must be together regularly and often – infants to octogenarians.'[88] The Old Testament image of feasting is helpful here: gathering around a meal where all are welcome, which is not rigidly structured but offers freedom and space to be a godly tribe.

2 Building relationships

Encouraging different age groups to get to know each other may not always run smoothly. As Menconi highlights, people born in different eras have different beliefs and experiences that will impact on how they engage with others.[89] Tensions are inevitable. Different generations will view life and faith through a distinct lens, and we need to be alert to this. Through the simple act of conversation, however, it's possible to build understanding of what it may mean to be older or younger. Menconi's project, in which different generations shared their stories, had a profound impact on growing cross-generational empathy and erasing misunderstanding. Through both formal and informal times to converse, we can deepen friendships and create new ones in often unexpected places. This encourages interdependence and a sense of being family that goes beyond assumed ideas or the stereotypes of the nuclear family, to a place where new ties and 'families' might be created in which everyone is able to find a place of belonging.

The Generations Working Together project in Scotland has brought together older and younger people in a fun competition, 'The Intergenerational Quiz'. This innovative idea has meant young and old alike can get to know each other better, recognising the contribution that each can make for the benefit of everyone on the team.

Opportunities for mission, for service and to work alongside each other in the life of the church are vital, and we need to pursue ways to do this that bring people of different ages together. By working with others on a task or project we get to know each other, as well as learn how others operate or approach activities of this nature. Emery-Wright and Mackenzie point to the transformative nature of this kind of ministry for young people especially.[90] This transformation can occur for all those involved at some level, whether in bringing new understanding or developing spiritually.

3 Enhancing worship

There can often be something mysterious and intangible about the times we gather in worship as all ages. Coming before God to worship him and learn together is a key part of what it means to be a disciple. When the room is full of every age group, at worst it's like a rowdy melee, but at best it's a joyful life-affirming gathering. It might be daunting to actively pursue intergenerationality in this context, but not if we take time to consider how to ensure they're meaningful – worshipful – times for everyone, regardless of age.

That probably means ditching our preconceived notions of 'all-age services', which in reality have become painful for everyone involved. Instead let's consider our language and how we're able to explain the nature of church, its rites and rituals, so that everyone is able to understand and participate to their fullest. Bird talks about moving from 'jargon' to 'signposts' – finding means to communicate effectively to everyone. She suggests thinking of simple verbal, visual and kinesthetic signposts that, when used consistently, are beneficial for all.[91] There's a need to reflect on how we can blend styles of worship that will enable everyone to participate.[92]

Becoming an intergenerational church goes beyond considering it as a programme to implement. It is more a mindset to approaching church life and activity in such a way that everyone, regardless of age, can access and feel a part of the 'tribe' or community, able both to receive support when necessary and to serve for the benefit of others. It's about each member, from the youngest to the eldest, recognising they are part of community with others and having an opportunity to actively participate.

To help you become an intergenerational church, I recommend two books. In *Intergenerational Christian Formation*, Allen and Ross offer a range of creative ideas that allow faith communities to explore scripture, worship together, share stories and build relationships. These suggestions provide a springboard to creating opportunities relevant for your own context and different age groups. Chapter 5 of *Generations Together*, by Kathie Amidei, Jim Merhaut and John Roberto, contains an essential congregational toolkit with a wealth of ideas and starting points for nurturing intergenerational church life. Organised under the headings of caring, celebrating, learning, praying and serving, there's a vast array of ways to bring different age groups together intentionally that connect church, home and life.[93]

Conclusion

This exploration of a host of intergenerational thinking and practice is intrinsic to how we approach ministry with families. Our work and support almost always have an age element to them that we can't afford to ignore. When we proactively seek to gather generations in meaningful ways, the benefits can be enormous, not only for individuals and families but also for the wider church.

This chapter has been something of a whistle-stop tour of what it means to be an intergenerational church community. My aim has been to stimulate your own contextual reflections and offer avenues to explore further. Yet it's important to emphasise that transitioning to becoming a church with an intergenerational foundation isn't necessarily a simple or an easy process; there are often barriers that are difficult to overcome and new understandings and relationships that need to be created and invested in for the long-term work of greater generational life together. It requires a cultural shift and a need to adopt a whole new ethos and vision that influences our mission and purpose as believers together.

This doesn't mean that everything needs to be intergenerational – all ages together all the time. There still need to be occasions when gathering as specific age groups is vital and valuable. Peer group time, whether in large or small groups, should form part of the diversity that church life offers. Being intergenerational in our thinking requires us to become more intentional when we do come together, whether socially or in worship and mission.

Embracing a model of being church of all ages requires determination and long-term resolve to move in this direction, recognising that we are all, regardless of age, travelling on a road of faith, learning as we go. As Allen and Ross declare:

> Truly intergenerational communities welcome children, emerging adults, recovering addicts, single adults, widows, single parents, teens whose parents are not around, the elderly, those in crisis, empty nesters and struggling parents of young children into a safe but challenging place to be formed into the image of Christ.[94]

Questions for reflection

- What different generations do you have in your church and community?

- Where do you identify your church as being on the spectrum between multigenerational and intergenerational?

- Where are the 'meeting points' where different generations already interact with each other?

- Where might be the best starting point for your church's movement into becoming a more intergenerational community? Who might you need to have conversations with to make this happen?

8

BE MISSIONAL

Introduction

What does the term 'missional family' conjure up for you? Maybe an image of dedicated, radical, evangelical parents – dyed-in-the-wool Christians – who have uprooted themselves and their family for the sake of the gospel to settle in another nation, taking the bold step to bring a witness to a new community by living among them – a family whose faith is so solid and unshakeable only they could embark on such an intrepid quest. They are unique, especially holy families, a breed set apart (as we perceive them), able to relinquish their home comforts to be obedient followers of Christ.

On closer inspection, the notion of becoming a missional family has much to excite and challenge each one of us. What if we were able to nurture families' sense of being on mission in the place where they live? Or what if we could raise the missional dimension of the ministry we're doing in local settings? It could be transformational for parents, carers, children and their extended families. It may not culturally be easy for Christian families in the UK to embrace the evangelical edge of their life together, but it's a dimension of discipleship that's well worth exploring and understanding better.

The *We Are Family* research project identified that much of what those who work with families do could be termed 'missional': it is outward-focused and seeks to put faith into action and demonstrate the enormous generosity of God's love. This missional aspect of family ministry, however, is often underplayed – it happens almost by accident or is reined in for fear of offending families who don't want to participate in activities they perceive as 'religious'. The evangelical edge to so much that family practitioners do tends to be restricted or limited. Yet surely there's a strong case to be made for rediscovering the missional dynamic of working with families.

In the great commission (Matthew 28:19–20) we have a powerful call from Jesus to reach out to those around us with the good news. We're called to 'go and make disciples of all the nations' – that is, following our own discovery of grace and the vast, overwhelming love that God has for us, we are to go and be a blessing to others. The story of Jesus' ministry reflects this impetus for God's love to be made known – scripture describes many occasions when people found their lives being transformed by Christ's words and deeds. The same task falls to us as his followers to be people willing to share this power and goodness, extending love to the world around us.

In contemporary theology, the biblical portrayal of God's mission – his call on us to join in with all that he is committed to doing in his world – is summed up in the term 'Missio Dei'. This concept 'traces mission as a theme throughout the whole Bible and points to the importance of a holistic mission that reflects God's reconciling work in creation as well as redemption'.[95] Missio Dei recognises that mission is not a silo activity, bolted on to the myriad other aspects of our discipleship; rather it permeates our day-to-day lives, naturally overflowing and being expressed in all aspects of our work, life and relationships with others.

Transferring this understanding to family ministry can overhaul narrow understandings of what mission is and how it occurs and the perception that it is a task for a select few. We can view the missional lives of families within the wider dimension of how a church adopts a missional approach in the locality they move and serve in. This places a church's congregation within the wider community. Diana Garland helpfully illustrates this with concentric circles, where the congregation sits within a local neighbourhood, which sits within the larger circle of the rest of the world.

There are two dimensions here. The first explores routes into taking a missional approach via all the various activities and events a church provides for those who live in the surrounding area: a toddler group, a summer picnic for families or sessions that provide specific family support – all of which offer opportunities to share elements of faith and the gospel. The second dimension is through cultivating a family's own sense of being 'on mission', that through their own life and witness they can display to friends and family what it can look like to follow Jesus. These two dimensions can require different kinds of equipping, organisation and support but are importantly underpinned by the same principles.

Mission can be embedded into our ministry with children, parents, carers, young people and their extended families in a variety of unique and innovative ways. In this chapter, we'll explore how adopting a missional approach can be of benefit to those we engage with across our church and broader communities, considering ways to shape our missional practice to and with them as well as fostering a desire in families themselves to embrace their own missional purpose.

Missional ministry

What compels us to pursue a missional life, one that is intentional about sharing faith, presenting the gospel and putting God centre stage? Our motivation and impetus are drawn from Jesus' example, whose 'own (earthly) mission was one of missiological engagement'.[96] Jesus brought together words and deeds through his love and concern, particularly for those on the fringes of society. He didn't set out purely to heal physical illness or feed the hungry, meeting only people's physical needs. He saw the whole person and drew together the differing dimensions of their being.

When Jesus encountered the woman at the well (John 4), their conversation extended beyond her thirst for fresh water to her need for living water that would satisfy her deep spiritual longing. It's an encounter that's about both a drink and an opportunity to hear the good news that can lead to an altogether different life.

Jesus knew that the physical demands of our existence, such as a decent meal and a roof over our head, were important, but he urged us to fix our eyes on our soul needs:

> Do not set your heart on what you will eat and drink; do not worry about it… Provide purses for yourselves that will not wear out, a treasure in heaven that will never fail, where no thief comes near and no moth destroys. For where your treasure is, there your heart will be also.
>
> LUKE 12:29, 33–34 (NIV)

Jesus recognised the inextricable links between the physical and the spiritual nature of being human. Jesus encountered people in their daily lives, responded to their presenting needs and questions in ways that transformed their sense of identity and self, and remedied the practical struggles they faced. For him the two went hand-in-hand, never one without the other, and this provides us with a powerful, lasting example of the form our own missional ministry should take.

Mission is a holistic activity. It draws together all the diverse elements of our being human: the spiritual, social, economic, physical, emotional and mental, working towards meeting the needs of mind, body and soul. When considering the shape of a missional family ministry, we can follow this same path, one that doesn't aim to address just one aspect of human need but rather views the holistic needs families have, both as a collective and as individuals. Through our ministry activity, it's possible to interweave these duel strands – if given careful thought, they need not be distinct or separate. We can offer practical support *and* bring good news at the same time.

To do this might require us to rethink the shape of our ministry and practice – what might it look like if we overlaid these aspects and took a more holistic approach? Rather than hosting one-off 'evangelistic' events or extending an invitation to a specific church service, could there be more intentional times to speak of faith during toddler group? In those seasons of celebration during the Christian calendar, such as Christmas and Easter, could we offer moments of reflection on their significance? When meeting someone's dire need for practical help, are we able to offer a moment to pray for them and their circumstances? As people from our local communities enter and meet in church buildings for all kinds of activities, where do they see faith expressed or defined? Sometimes the eyes of someone without expressed faith can powerfully reveal to us the experience of being in a building that reflects nothing of the community which worships there; looking objectively at our spaces and facilities can help create more missionally welcoming environments. The sign outside may say 'welcome', but does what is encountered inside convey the same message? In essence, 'a strong case can be made for seeing mission as involving both evangelism and good works, loving others and seeking to "bless" all in the world'.[97]

We need to be less anxious about speaking of faith and God in those places not immediately seen as worshipping or spiritual settings. When our faith is rooted in the everyday, mundane routines of life as well as in the gathered times of worship, we can become more able to express our thanks, remorse and prayerful cries of hope that demonstrate our ongoing commitment to following in Jesus' footsteps. In God's strength we can develop the language and ability to speak of him in honest ways. He equips us for the work of ministry and urges us to bear witness to him in the thick of it. Mission is equally transformative for us as believers, as we engage in demonstrating God's love in the world, as it is for those we're striving to reach.

When we're looking to adopt a stronger missional approach, it needs to be one that's holistic, built on the following understanding:

- *Reflect the context* – Stepping into mission will always have a strong contextual basis. The place we find ourselves provides the parameters for what shape our mission activity will take. If it doesn't start with the people and issues that matter locally, it's unlikely to have much of an impact. We let our surroundings be the basis for how we serve and share the gospel in the places we live.

- *Authenticity is valued* – We should display a willingness to be fully ourselves in the reality of where we are in life. It isn't about presenting an ideal or striving to show that life is rosy and we're perfect. Instead we're aware that God exists with us in the mess that day-to-day life often is, in our struggles and challenges, and in the questions we have about who he is, how he operates and how we try to make sense of that in the world we live in. Authentic faith is a life lived removing the masks we often wear and revealing our humanity in the midst of pursuing relationship with God.

- *Family need is multidimensional* – As we reflected earlier, family life is often complex, and each family will have its own needs and concerns. These are often practical in nature and require practical support in response, but it's important to give time and thought to how the spiritual dimension of their lives isn't neglected in the midst of doing this.

- *Start with families* – Keeping our experience and knowledge of the families we meet and work with in the foreground is key. It's the building block of so much of what we do in family ministry, and that includes when we embark on developing missional activities and ideas.

- *Join with others* – There is a strong case to be made for always looking for others – churches, congregations, organisations and agencies – to collaborate with, especially when considering new missional ventures. Don't go it alone!

In many of our congregations it is likely that there are families who recognise the relevance of the great commission in their own lives, those who see the significance of being people who reach beyond church circles and engage with others, sharing the gospel and the impact it makes on the lives of those who follow Jesus. Yet for many the notion of being on mission as a family group may be an unfamiliar concept. As I said earlier, it may come as news to them that this is something that takes place in the neighbourhoods around our homes. They might not grasp that, as Scott Douglas says, 'the mission field isn't only a faraway place that requires passports and immunisations'.[98] Mission doesn't have to mean a costly trip abroad; it can take the form of expressions of faith and love that are right on our doorstep.

Missional families

So how can we support families to imagine new ways to be on mission in their usual localities and settings? Douglas believes that families are mission agencies in their own right and that this can begin at home. For some it may take a lot to persuade them out of their comfort zone, but taking small steps in this direction can build confidence and equip families. By reflecting on some simple questions, families can begin identifying ways to become more missional:

- What are the issues we care about? Where would we like to bring about change, however small?

- What gifts and talents do we have, both individually and collectively? How could we use these to share the gospel?

- Where are the places we know of that we could support, both locally and globally?

- What are the organisations, charities or agencies that we might be able to become involved with, both nearby and further afield?

- Who else do we know, who might be able to help us or share similar interests, who may want to be involved?

These questions give parents, carers, children, young people and maybe their extended families a chance to reflect on their own unique circumstances and what they have to offer. It helps them build an approach to mission all their own and that can be embedded into their circumstances. It offers an opportunity to consider who else they could join with – maybe other groups that share their compassion and desire to change the world in that specific way. Their goal may be grand or simple, but it presents a way to be missionally and meaningfully engaged in the world they live in. As family ministry practitioners, we can support the approach they take, offering advice where needed as well as encouragement and prayerful support.

When our boys were younger, we were fortunate to know a number of like-minded families who wanted to find ways to bless and care for our neighbourhood. In simple ways, such as Sunday morning litter-picking or 'stop and pray' walks through our local streets, we spent time with other parents, their children and in fact anyone who wanted to join us, including single people and grandparents without family living locally. Through our time together we created a sense of being extended family for each other, and different ages were able to develop understanding of what it might look like to serve and live out our faith. In conjunction with others we sought to find ways to adopt the great commission in our familiar roads and pavements. We wanted to be a blessing, taking the church beyond the walls of its building and our faith beyond the walls of our homes.

Through the process of generating a missional view, families can have an impact on the place where they live but also on each other and on their views and understanding of the people and world around them. Douglas suggests four things that committing to becoming a missional family might change:[99]

- *Greater communication* – In the process of making and discussing plans, there are opportunities to share ideas, for all members of the family to be heard and contribute to what their specific mission is going to look like. The basis of their project may be personal interests, passions or experiences, which means it reflects who they are as family and increases their own sense of identity. As they make progress and their work takes shape, as everyone has a chance to be involved, new aspects of each other can be discovered. When a project comes to fruition there's the opportunity to celebrate all that's been accomplished, which isn't limited solely to the outcomes of their mission but also to how they also recognise the impact on them as a family.

- *Launch of a missions legacy that lasts for generations* – As families begin to embed a missional way of life into their everyday living, it offers the foundation of a life that will perpetuate as children grow and become adults themselves. For some there's the definite possibility that this becomes the core activity of their being as family – one that dictates the choices they make about how they live. I've known many children who, having had missional experiences with their parents and carers, become passionate missionaries on their own doorsteps, characterised by a boldness that opens their eyes to all the possibilities around them.

- *Cultivation of compassion for our community and world* – A key component of embarking on missional activity is a willingness to step into the struggles and suffering of others. Seeing in the world around us how people struggle with a variety of issues, such as poverty, exploitation, mental health and environmental degradation, develops our empathy and raises understanding of God's love and concern for the world and people he created. Viewing tough circumstances through a divine lens can challenge our prejudices, helping us to embrace our common humanity and reduce a sense of 'us' and 'them'. As our compassion grows, we can explore ways to creatively respond, both practically and spiritually, as we reach out to care for others.

- *Renewed recognition of God's purpose for families* – Engaging in activities that share the gospel and meet people's physical need can be a powerful reminder of our calling. For families, this can bring people together of different ages and stages of their faith journeys in a way that proves to be transformative. It reminds us, too, that through working together we can make change happen – even in just small ways – and that each of our contributions makes a difference. God uses our differing abilities and skills to aid others, regardless of our age. The combined impact a family has together reminds us that we each have a part to play in God's mission across the globe.

Looking at the entire spectrum of church life and identifying the opportunities for parents and children to participate and serve together can be a helpful starting point, especially if these offer ways for children to participate at an early age so that ideas of being missional are firmly embedded as shared activity. Churches support families by creating a climate that nurtures their becoming missional and support them to take the first steps. Beginning by building relationships with our literal neighbours – those living on the same street – is a superb way to begin. Being hospitable, getting to know those on our doorsteps and considering ways to be kind and helpful can foster a sense of reaching out beyond our own four walls. Families' confidence can grow enormously as they talk more about faith and share the gospel, something children can often be much more at ease with and comfortable doing than adults.

Developing a language to speak of faith in this way is key; as families grow as disciples together, they're able to build this. Learning to put into words what we believe shapes us to become missionally leaning people. Children and young people can often lead the way for adults in doing this. As Jonathan Williams helpfully reminds us, there should always be room for passion – what he describes as 'gospel boldness': 'See the passion of our children and, instead of pushing it back… cultivate it, encourage it, and lead our children to become passionate and bold for the things of Christ!'[100]

Where there are pre-existing connections with individuals and families on mission in places further afield, the church can provide opportunities to share what they're doing and to regularly pray for them. Growing this sense of 'there and here' enhances our missional edges, often shrinking the world in the process, so we're able to identify the shared challenges and joys it can bring.

We need to take care in exploring ways for everyone to participate. Being inclusive is vital, as otherwise we're in danger of conveying that this kind of mission engagement is only for certain kinds of families. We run the risk of excluding those who may not feel they fit the traditional forms of families or that mission can only be undertaken by those in a nuclear family. We do well to bear in mind ways to intentionally include children whose parents or carers aren't followers of Jesus, single people and those who are widowed or divorced. They need to be 'enfolded into families', as Douglas describes, where they find a place to belong, serve, contribute and share in the God-given commission we share.[101] Giving careful consideration to how our activities may include or exclude is worth doing beforehand so everyone is able to access the opportunities on offer.

Finally our approach to being people 'on mission' is important. Planning may be thorough and enthusiasm high, but if our attitudes aren't right a great deal of harm can be done. There is a strong possibility that if we 'treat such experiences as tourists rather than pilgrims',[102] much of what we strive to accomplish can be lost. Rather than being passive observers, we need to be fully invested disciples walking alongside others, committed to giving of ourselves in ways that demonstrate our empathy and shared humanity. Mission that encourages families to be authentic and demonstrate a meaningful working out of the gospel reflects a living hope to be shared wherever our feet take us.

Conclusion

Hopefully by now you're persuaded that raising the missional bar for the ministry you're engaged in is enormously important. If you're still unsure whether it's even possible I hope you are nevertheless willing to give it a go, at least in a small way. Who knows where that might lead? Alas, the word 'mission' has become unfashionable and uncomfortable for many in family ministry. It's been a neglected area, but there are indications that the tide is turning – with a generation of unchurched adults now becoming parents, there's renewed curiosity about the faith rituals and rites of passage for Christians. They're discovering for the first time the stories some of us take for granted, learning about a man from Nazareth and his heavenly Father who have nothing but genuine, life-transforming purposes in mind for us. For many people, there's a mismatch between their perception of the Christian faith and the reality they encounter. The more we can bring this life-giving message to people through our family ministry activity, the greater hope exists of lives reinvigorated by coming face-to-face with the God who loves them unconditionally. Let's put aside some of the fear or anxiety of being open and upfront about our beliefs and basis of faith, and instead discover simple and fun new ways of incorporating it into the very basis of our work.

As we raise the profile of our missional intention, as families come to recognise the call on them to serve and also become bringers of good news, we may see a new generation excited to courageously step out of their comfort zones. Being missional people brings an opportunity to embed the great commission as a lived experience and practice. Yet it requires more than simply learning about other people and cultures; it has the potential to profoundly shift our view of the world and change us deeply. As Steven Emery-Wright and Ed Mackenzie declare: 'It requires inward transformation, a transformation that sees others as loved by God. Prejudices, stereotypes and unquestioned assumptions of other people are challenged when we meet real people of other cultures and faiths.' They go on to say how it shapes our 'cultural intelligence… the ability to empathize with and so more deeply love those who are different than us'.[103] This is surely why the calling Jesus made on our lives as his followers is so significant, as it contains the prospect of seeing change within ourselves as well as within those we come into contact with.

Our missional lives are intrinsically woven into our broader faith and personal development, the people we are becoming as we follow Jesus. We are able to not only support families in bringing about change in their homes, communities and places further afield, but also see change take place in them, their beliefs, their relationship with God and their ongoing walk together as disciples. And this is all possible because we know that God makes it possible. He dwells with us, empowers us and travels with us as we take those steps of faith with him. It draws us to the striking image depicted in Isaiah 54, which we can read through a missional lens:

> Enlarge the place of your tent,
>   stretch your tent curtains wide,
>   do not hold back;
> lengthen your cords,
>   strengthen your stakes.
> For you will spread out to the right and to the left;
>   your descendants will dispossess nations
>   and settle in their desolate cities.
> ISAIAH 54:2–3 (NIV)

Here the prophet urges us to have confidence in God's covenant and unfailing love, to step out, compelled to both be and share good news among all we know and meet. Let's wonder about the possibilities if our families were to catch this vision and pursue it to the ends of the earth!

Questions for reflection

- How far could you describe your ministry and practice as being missional?

- Where are the opportunities in your current activities and programmes to share the gospel more openly?

- What might be some of the barriers for you and your church in doing this?

9

BE HOLY AT HOME

Introduction

My early days of parenting are a bit of a blur – especially all these years later as my offspring are on the brink of becoming adults – but I have some recollections: changing nappies, feedings, trips to the local park, afternoon naps (for them and me), reading stories and tired cuddles at the end of the day. When children are young, parenting is intense – a demanding physical activity to meet their every need. No one ever truly grasps how demanding those early weeks and months are until they find themselves in the thick of them. Caring at this point is fully immersive and all-consuming – the tiny humans we've created are the centre of our world. For me, my understanding of what it means to love, realising I'd give and do anything for my children, was profoundly changed.

Having children changed me personally, as I was brought face-to-face with what it meant to be a parent. To provide for my children, to protect and nurture them, to raise them in a way that would launch them well into adulthood – my responsibilities loomed large at times. Yet day in, day out, I simply strived to do my best, seeking to rely on God to fill the gaps and do the things I couldn't do, to provide the energy I didn't have or to grow my confidence in my parenting skills. I wonder if any of this sounds familiar.

During this time there was a dawning realisation that beyond my human, practical role lay a spiritual one. This thought began small, a tiny seed of an idea which then grew and grew. Beyond being a provider for my sons, I also had a role to play in nurturing their awareness of God's presence, with us at home and in the world around us. I wanted them to grow knowing that he was with us, recognising him day by day at work in our lives and beyond. I hoped that during their childhood they would encounter him in refreshing awe and wonder. But where on earth to start? What might it look like for our home to be a place where faith grew and was shared? My early parenting was greatly influenced by my own upbringing, which I imagine is true for many of us. Yet having come from a home where Christian practices weren't an everyday experience, I was clueless about how to lay spiritual foundations for us as a family of four. This was the beginning of my own venture into learning about what discipleship at home could look like, exploring some of the approaches and understanding more of what the phrase 'faith at home' meant. It was a true voyage of discovery, and our boys were very much guinea pigs along the way.

It soon dawned on me that I wasn't the only parent curious about what the six days beyond church services looked like at home from a faith perspective. Conversations with others revealed how many of us were wondering how to do this. So as a practitioner I began to consider the role I had to play in offering support and raising the profile of being a family of faith at home. My interest has never waned since. It's fascinating to see that as ministry to families has risen up the agenda over the past decade, so has our curiosity around faith at home and the part the church has to play in equipping parents, children and young people to grow in discipleship together. In this chapter we'll spend time understanding why faith matters at home and exploring the role of family ministry practitioners in supporting parents in this vital aspect of raising their children.

A culture of holiness

In *Postmodern Children's Ministry*, Ivy Beckwith explores the nature of children's faith formation and makes a strong case for this needing to be a collective activity:

> God surrounded children with adults both in the extended biological family and the community of faith for a reason. Parents and other adults are there to guide, teach, and model life for our children. Not only are we to teach things like how to button a button, use a spoon, and throw a baseball, but we are also to pass on the things of God and Jesus through our relationships with these children.[104]

For Beckwith the responsibilities of parenting and caregiving go far beyond the practical tasks and nurturing of skills into cultivating children's spiritual lives, recognising that this dimension of life is just as, if not more, important than everything else we can contribute to their being. As much as faith is a participatory activity when people gather for the Sunday church service, so it is back in the home when family members gather as what Roman Catholic educators call a 'domestic church'.

So what do we mean by 'faith at home' or 'family faith'? Both are terms we are hearing more and more, to which we might have a range of responses: excitement, trepidation, curiosity. This either hinders or propels us to explore what it could look like for our own families. If we've had good experiences ourselves, that undoubtedly helps, but if we have no experience or an unhelpful one, we may feel more wary of engaging with a topic that feels vast and undefined.

The sense of 'lived holiness' we read of in Micah (see chapter 2, page 37) provides a useful starting point for thinking about the home and seeking to lay holiness as a foundation to family life, but how do we approach doing this? What might a culture of holiness look like at home? It's about:

- adopting practices, such as the way we worship with each other, pray or read scripture.
- embedding attitudes and values, such as fostering generous natures and learning to be respectful of each other.

It's about, over time, interweaving these two things into the ebb and flow of our day-to-day life as family – waking up, getting ready for work and school and travelling to and from these places; the people we meet, work with and learn alongside; the conversations we have and the things we observe; the after-school activities and sports we might participate in; the evening meal we share together; and the winding down after hectic days towards our bedtime routines and rituals. There are a thousand and one possibilities contained within what may seem mundane or everyday habits, journeys and experiences.

We can support and encourage families to be alert to the multitude of ways they may encounter God and join in with what he's doing. These might have their focus in family devotional times. As parents model these things, as we encounter them on a regular basis, they become part of our daily lived experience and impact on our values, the decisions we make and why, and how we interact with one another as well as others in the wider world. Early on perhaps we'll need to be more explicit about the when and the why, but as time passes there's less need to do this. It is important to understand this as a whole family – as much as parents may initially introduce and encourage, it's not about 'teaching' children but about sharing in developing these things together. So there's a mutual accountability in our discipleship.

According to Ed Mackenzie and Gareth Crispin, as well as a host of other writers and researchers, there are two key elements to worshipping as a family: listening to God and talking to God.[105] Our listening includes reading scripture, mulling it over and together asking questions about what we're reading: why did that happen? Who's this person we're reading about? Why did they act in that way? What do I learn about God from this? This grows our understanding, helps us discover new things and recognises that passages mean different things to different people; we don't all read or hear it in the same way. By having these conversations, everyone in a family has the opportunity to participate to the extent of their own understanding. We're at different ages and stages in life and faith.

Our talking to God occurs through prayer and the conversations we have with him in a host of different times and places, sometimes on a more formal basis, for instance via liturgy in a church service or set prayer times in our daily routines, and also informally as we travel to school or work, cry out at moments of distress or worry or thankfulness. Families can experiment with what suits them. When my boys were younger, we regularly said prayers at bedtime, bringing all the events of our day to God, asking for help for the following day, recognising those times when he'd been with us and giving thanks for all the ways he'd taken care of us.

Praying together involves developing the notion of us being in dialogue with God. As much as we want to share the things that matter to us, we also need to learn to listen to him. These prayer times have the potential to become meaningful milestones in our daily lives: times when we're able to bring the full messiness of our lives before God, to be reminded of his glory and to be built up in our faith and trust that he's always with us.

Ten tips for family devotional times

Families can be daunted by the prospect of putting time aside that has a specific faith and worship focus – they may feel ill-equipped or that the expectations for doing something of this nature are too high. Here are some pointers to use when reassuring them in cultivating a life of faith.

1   Find a time in the day that works for you.

2   Don't expect it to be a silent and reverential time; it will be messy! Children will say and do unexpected things, so try to go with the flow.

3   Encourage everyone to contribute. Don't let it become a time when the adults do all the talking and children are expected to listen.

4   Be flexible. Don't try to keep to a strict plan, and do something different now and again.

5   Be adaptable. As children grow let the time together evolve in new ways, involve everyone and recognise that everyone's thoughts and ideas matter. What works for a family with young children isn't going to be fit for those with teenagers.

6   Explore using different resources if that proves a helpful place to start (see Additional Resources at the end of this book).

7   Use the day's events to explore where you've each met with God or seen him at work. Let these things encourage and build one another up.

8   Let the Christian seasons of the year provide a path for your family worship time, for instance in the run-up to Christmas or Easter.

9   Be ready to see things differently. Our life experience will always colour how we see and experience God; enjoy getting to know how others in your family find this.

10   Watch the time. Some days everyone will gladly hang around together, have a lot to say and fill the time with purpose. Other days there'll be fidgeting, interruptions and distractions, so don't be so determined to see it through that everyone is left frustrated or resentful.

Diana Garland builds on these notions of families experiencing faith together, defining it as 'shared beliefs and values about what is most important in life, expressed and shaped in shared family activity'.[106] That is, faith is more than what we believe and the values we adopt; it's also expressed in and through our actions. There's an outward movement from the ways we nurture faith as a daily habit (our practices) to how these influence what we find important in life (our values and attitudes) to how that faith is demonstrated through our actions and engagement with the world around us (our mission). This is summed up in a beautiful phrase that Garland uses: 'sacred stories' – in other words, the ways families live out their faith together in diverse forms. This connects what happens within households – worship, learning and wondering – with what we do in the communities and environments we live in.

In this, the idea of 'service' is crucial. Rick Rusaw and Eric Swanson speak of church as a 'place of rehabilitation, not convalescence'.[107] Read through a family ministry lens, this also applies to Christian families. What a powerful image! The church is a place that reforms and equips us to go into the world to make a difference for God's sake; equally our homes can do the same for those who dwell there. For this to happen it often requires elements of our faith to be drawn together, such as prayer and reading scripture. Providing opportunities for children to apply faith through service from their early years embeds their faith as they grow into teenagers and young adults. Not doing so risks a growing disconnect arising between our beliefs and Christian faith on paper and what they look like in practice or in action. Bringing these together provides an effective means by which we make sense of what we believe and grow in our understanding.

Ten tips for families serving together

Encouraging families to serve with each other can take a wide variety of forms, but there are some simple tips regardless of how they may choose to do this:

1   Choose something to which everyone can make a contribution, however big or small.

2   Be willing to try something before fully committing to it.

3   Give everyone in the family a chance to share how they found it; let everyone's views be valued.

4   Give thought beforehand to issues of child safety and security; ask further questions if necessary.

5   Agree to a regular opportunity to serve together, whether that is weekly, monthly, annually or somewhere in between. Do what works best for your family.

6   Recognise that as much as you have something to offer, your family also has a great deal to learn while serving or on mission together.

7   Discover if there are other families interested in what you're doing; see if they'll join you or are keen to develop a joint project or way of serving.

8   Recognise that there will inevitably be times when not everyone in the family 'feels like' going or contributing; try to minimise pressure to participate beyond what feels comfortable.

9   Be led by the interests you have as a family and the gifts each member has; find ways to serve that put them to good use.

10   Be prayerful – before you go, while you're there and when you return home.

Supporting family faith

Some years back, when I was first musing over the intriguing concept of families growing in faith, I came across a book that has been enormously influential on my thinking and practice ever since. *Think Orange* by Reggie Joiner argues that something great comes when churches and families work together.[108] He points out that each year a church has 40 hours in which it might influence a child's life, but parents and carers have 3,000. This floored me! Why weren't we thinking more about what happens in the home? Orange continues to be a movement dedicated to equipping churches, their leaders and parents to work together, recognising that something bigger and more impactful can be accomplished if we do so.

If you're a practitioner, you have a vital role to play. Being an encouraging and supportive influence on families as they journey in faith together is essential to who you are and what you do. Joining them on this voyage of faith discovery – whether introducing them to the gospel, responding to their questions, exploring Christian festivals and rites of passage or rooting faith more deeply through worship and service – is vital to your ministry. It's something you need to consider integrating into the vast array of activity you're involved in. Make it a high priority.

Much of how we opt to approach this will depend on the kind of families in our churches and communities. We'll want to tailor what we do to their needs and expressed hopes. By recognising the importance of faith and striving to reduce the gap between Sunday services and what happens in homes, essential connections can be made. As Beckwith says, 'Perhaps the best tool we can give parents is to relieve them of the belief that this is rocket science.'[109]

How can we intentionally foster this and keep it simple too?

- *Be an equipper* – Many of the parents, grandparents and carers in our church communities may feel they simply don't have the skills or knowledge to integrate faith in their day-to-day lives. It may seem too daunting, they may not have experienced it themselves or they may feel it's something only the 'super-spiritual' can ever do. We need to work hard to dispel these myths, build confidence, nurture enthusiasm and equip them to lay the foundations of being a family of faith bit by bit. We can helpfully model some approaches when we're in church together, giving families a chance to try them out, putting time aside in worship services to do this as well as generating resources to take away that will support families when they discuss faith matters at home.

- *Be a connector* – Find ways to draw a link between what happens in church and back at home. This may include using language that frequently refers to this, so that families begin to make greater associations. Encourage honest conversations around home life (e.g. the challenges of finding time to gather and explore faith together – to actually do it) and provide opportunities for parents and carers to share openly about their experiences when praying or reading the Bible. It is easy to make assumptions that everyone else is doing it better than we are, so it's essential to keep these going. Be willing to listen when family faith times aren't going well at home, as much as celebrating with families when things are going well.

- *Be a supporter* – Help families to know that nurturing faith at home is definitely possible yet will probably look different for everyone. No one approach is going to suit every family. There may be a need to experiment with different times and methods. We need to correct the false assumption that being a family of faith is only for nuclear families and be proactive in sharing the possibilities for all kinds of different forms of family. Parenting today can often feel a very scrutinised activity, so let's not add to parents' fears or let them feel that family discipleship is another pressure or burden in life.

- *Be an inventor* – Think imaginatively and help families see the possibilities. We might need to help them dream and be reminded of the calling of Deuteronomy 6 (see chapter 2, page 34). There isn't a one-size-fits-all approach, so let your creativity be the only limitation. Growing faith together can happen at home, on holiday, outdoors, during the school run, in the car – anywhere we are can be a place to meet with God. Nurture this limitless approach. There's a wealth of published resources now that can be useful for families when doing this. We may be guided by the seasons, by events in our lives or by news about the wider world, and our faith time together as a family gives an opportunity to reflect and explore these things more. It may be helpful to gather from families ideas that they've tried and let them be the generator of great resources that others can tap into too.

- *Be in it too* – Let's be prepared to share our own experiences and be honest when stuff doesn't work – it helps families to see that others are trying and not always getting it right. There is, however, a balance to be struck when sharing our personal circumstances – it may not be fair on our own children to always make them the example. But being able to recognise some of the challenges involved, and some of the lessons we've learnt along the way, can be an encouraging factor to others on the same road.

Many of us will undoubtedly have a breadth of relationships with families: unique connections with different parents, carers and grandparents, some of whom we've known for years and others who have only recently moved into the area; those we see frequently and regularly, and others who drop in now and again. Their faces may be familiar, but we'll know each and every one differently.

Joiner talks of these different 'levels of partnership': the *aware* (those outside the church but open to it and interested in developing their parenting); the *involved* (parents and carers engaged with church on the fringes, who participate occasionally); the *engaged* (those committed to working with the church and who are open to ideas of being spiritual leaders at home); and the *invested* (those being proactive in committing time to faith at home and partnering with the church to do this). He helpfully captures here the range of views, understanding and beliefs parents and carers may have about their spiritual role. It's worth considering for a moment where those in our settings, churches and communities might sit on this continuum. What do the levels of partnership with families look like where we are? What strategic steps might we need to take to deepen our partnership? It could be that starting with just one group in one part of your ministry could make a real difference to how families do faith together.

Faith at home resources

If you're looking for some additional support and ideas, there's an increasing range of resources available. Take a look at these three in particular, which have been raising the profile of nurturing faith at home in recent times:

The Kitchen Table Project

The Kitchen Table Project (**kitchentable.org.uk**) – an initiative of Care for the Family – followed some extensive research into how households develop faith together. Some of the key findings from this were:

- 95% of the parents surveyed acknowledged that it was largely their responsibility to teach their children about the Christian faith, and 78% of church leaders agreed with this.

- 36% of the parents surveyed felt very confident in nurturing their child's faith, whereas 26% felt not very confident. How confident a parent felt had a significant relationship to their views on nurturing faith and what they currently do at home.

- The main barrier to nurturing faith was felt to be that family time was devoted to other activities, or not having enough time with the child. This was followed by needing help with knowing what to do.

- Parents were keen to receive practical ideas for praying as a family and talking about faith at home.

So there was a clear sense that parents see faith at home as something they need to be doing but often lack confidence or face barriers to making it a reality in their homes. The Kitchen Table Project offers resources both for parents and carers and for churches, to encourage a sense of partnership between the two. A highlight from their website is the 'Inspire session', which is designed for parents and carers to meet in a small group to learn about adopting a faith-at-home approach and gain the confidence that they are the best people to do this. There's also a book, *Raising Faith* by Katharine Hill and Andy Frost, containing a wealth of ways to be intentional in growing as disciples together at home.

Parenting for Faith

Parenting for Faith (**parentingforfaith.org.uk**) – a ministry of The Bible Reading Fellowship – aims to equip parents and carers to raise God-connected children and teens by providing a broad array of resources developed out of Rachel Turner's book, *Parenting Children for a Life of Faith*.[110] It believes parents are perfectly positioned to disciple their children in the mundane, everyday bits of parenthood. But they can't do it alone, so there's a call to embed parents in networks with extended families and friends that are rooted in a church to strengthen and empower them in their call. It places a high value on utilising those everyday moments parents, carers and children share and not adding in extra activities. Parenting for Faith recognises that the adults in the home are those who are best placed to nurture faith and that as every family is unique, so too will be their journey of faith together – there's no one right way to do it!

On the website you can find a vast range of resources for both parents and churches, including the Parenting for Faith course. This contains eight video-based sessions designed to aid parents in discovering that they are in the ideal position to demonstrate the reality of a life with God to their children, empowering them to have their own vibrant two-way relationship with him.

GodVenture

An initiative of Victoria Beech, GodVenture (**godventure.co.uk**) offers an extensive array of creative resources that can be used equally well in the home or in playgroups. Among the prayer and scripture activities are those with a seasonal focus, taking advantage of the time of year to explore aspects of God's character and our relationship with him. Many of these ideas are superb opportunities to build faith into play, inviting children in to discover new things about God for themselves. Often using toys and items already found at home, GodVenture invites parents, carers and children into exciting new faith-based experiences with each other that prompt new learning, build relationships and deepen mutual understanding in the early years of children's lives.

Conclusion

In this chapter, we've sought to grapple with ideas of how we define being a 'family of faith' and the need for us to rediscover an ancient notion of discipleship being a family affair – that faith is worked out among people of different ages, that the young need the old and the old need the young to remain dedicated to the winding road of faith development. Parents, carers and grandparents are in a unique position to influence children's faith and to make it a joint enterprise, through which all our relationships with God are deepened.

Importantly, this is not to happen in isolation. Being gathered communities in church is important in shaping everyone's faith, as is the church's responsibility to help equip and affirm parents and carers as they establish their homes as places of faith. Those in lay and ordained ministry have a vital role reducing the gap between church and home, for one to extend into and influence the other, creating environments where faith for the other six days a week is a normal topic of conversation. We can provide resources, share stories of the highs and lows and work towards minimising their fears where holiness at home is concerned. Let's spur them on to see the surprising and simple ways to join God in what he's up to. There's so much more still to be done here that will influence faith for generations to come.

Day by day, week by week, month by month, family faith is fostered, enriched and nourished as parents, carers, children and young people are brought together in their walk with God. As they travel on this journey new traditions of faith are formed, with milestones and celebrations embedded into the lives of young and old. This becomes a family's story of faith. They are their own storytellers! They become part of the bigger story reflecting the glory of God, his faithfulness and desire to be known and made known, happening through both the minute and grand actions families take.

Holiness grows incrementally at home over time. It's about inviting God to come and dwell among us and choosing to live life in a way that honours him – but not by expecting to become perfect in the process or living life by a set of hard, inflexible rules. Instead holiness is a daily way of life that becomes interwoven in the million and one small and big things we do as God works his ongoing redemption in and through us. Holiness at home is a whole-family enterprise – a whole-church enterprise – and an exciting adventure of discovery that we embark on together.

Questions for reflection

- What was your experience of faith at home during your own childhood or teenage years? How does this help or hinder you in your own outlook?

- Reflect on these words from Micah 6: 'This is what he requires of you: to do what is right, to love mercy, and to walk humbly with your God.' What strikes a chord with you?

- How might you encourage families to recognise their 'sacred stories' of how they've grown in faith together?

- Are there opportunities for your families to serve together? If not how and where could you make these a reality?

- Identify some core families in your church with whom you could build partnerships that would support and equip them to grow in faith.

10

BE REFLECTIVE

Introduction

What does it mean to embrace reflective practice, and how do we define it? At a very simple level reflective practice is a tool. It helps us look at what we do and ask questions about how and why, as well as enabling us to improve and take steps to change ministry practice into the future. It provides an opportunity to make sense of and take meaning from our experiences. Rather than hurtling from one group and activity to the next, it requires us to pause and reflect back on what's taken place.

Reflective practice has its origins in the early 20th-century work of John Dewey, who described it in terms of considering what we believe and why. It has strong associations with professional contexts, such as education, social work, health and care. Reflective practice brings together our understanding of the work we do and the theory that exists around that work, along with our own wisdom and experience that develops over time. As Barbara Bassot asserts, 'It is not just pausing for thought from time to time... it is not a replacement for theory, but involves drawing on theory to enhance your understanding of practice; reflection, then, is a key means of applying theory to professional practice.'[111]

Reflective practice forms a kind of dialogue that invites questions to be asked and pondered on. It recognises that ministry is constantly evolving and aids us in establishing the best ways to shape the work that we do, with the families we know, in the places we find ourselves. As John Canavan, John Pinkerton and Pat Dolan state, adopting a reflective approach helps us 'to articulate what is being offered to families, why it is being offered, and how it will contribute to meeting the needs... of both parents and children'.[112] Therefore if we embrace a reflective approach, we have the potential to grasp a tool that will help us flourish and grow, one that places our individual ministries within the wider arena of both local church ministry and family ministry across the nation and beyond. This chapter will unpack more of what we mean when talking about being reflective practitioners and ways for us to take intentional steps that will be of benefit not only to us but also to the churches and communities we find ourselves serving in.

Reflective practice in ministry

How might reflective practice benefit our ministry? What might it have to offer our work that could enhance and develop it further? For many practitioners, our working lives can often be a complex juggling act of planning, preparing, managing and delivering; shifting from one group or session to the next; striving to ensure everything runs smoothly and nothing is forgotten. The nature of working in this way means there are rarely times set aside to reflect on what's actually taken place, how it may have been received and whether those participating found it to be beneficial to them. If we're able to embed reflective practices into our work, we can deepen our understanding of the approaches we take and consider why we do things the way we do and where we may wish to make changes in the future.

We may find that a particular group has run successfully with the same format for more than a decade, but interest appears to be dwindling and numbers are beginning to tail off. Instead of jumping to quick fixes or making temporary minor swaps, undertaking a time of reflection could identify some deeper issues that need addressing. It would question our assumptions of the right or best way to do something and highlight aspects we may previously have dismissed. We'd be more able to recognise that family ministry practice is always evolving and to adapt to these changes. Reflective practice can nurture our flexibility by acknowledging that there isn't one best approach but that, depending on circumstances, other options may be better suited.

Rarely in church ministry is it only our opinion that needs to be taken into consideration. On the contrary, often others seem to be intent on commenting on what we do. This can cause frustration and resentment, and it can be tempting to dismiss these other voices out of hand.

Reflective practice can support us to instead engage with these alternative perspectives, and it can provide a safe space for those different views to be more effectively unpacked and understood. Voices and opinions that previously may have been received as critical and unwelcome can be transformed towards becoming invaluable as they see ministry from an altogether different viewpoint. Nurturing those interested 'critical friends' – a small group who walk with us in ministry – can be a powerful tool in shaping practice with us.

Time after time during the *We Are Family* research project, we met workers who expressed a frequent sense of isolation in the work they did. Although they spent vast amounts of time with other people, on occasion their roles felt overwhelming and disjointed. Becoming a more reflective practitioner 'should encourage an holistic view on the part of the worker by which he or she takes into consideration the elements of programmes, the needs of the person being worked with and the role of all other relevant actors involved'.[113] This big-picture perspective isn't always easy to cultivate, especially among the day-to-day pressures of ministry. But if there are times to step back, we can piece together the various elements and develop a more cohesive sense of ministry.

Often what we may perceive as passing conversations or contact with parents, carers and families are in fact intrinsic to purposeful ministry. These might not be widely recognised practitioner skills or capabilities, but they're undoubtedly important day to day:

> Rather than seeing positive relationships as a given, there needs to be recognition that providing support to families requires considerable skills and expertise, and can be exhausting and stressful for the worker. Reflective practice is essential in order to ensure those who provide family support are aware of their professional and personal influence on those they work with.[114]

Have you ever paused to consider the skills, gifts and know-how you possess? Have you stopped to reflect on how you interact with people – the way you speak with them, the questions you ask and the way you respond? Often these abilities are woven into who we are; they seem to be natural aptitudes. What we don't see is how these have been honed and refined over the years through the frequent interactions we have. We instinctively respond to certain people and situations in certain ways, forgetting that this can still be tiring and cause us anxiety. Learning more about this aspect of ourselves, being honest about the stress points, helps us carry our ministry loads more effectively. It helps us to put down the things we need to and to share the burdens with others, and over time it builds us into more resilient, intentional practitioners.

Reflecting on practice can also be a powerful tool for evaluation. This can often be difficult in ministry environments. We may default to measuring the effectiveness of our work simply by counting how many people turned up and then comparing that number against previous attendance or against our hopes and expectations. Or we may look superficially at our initial intended outcomes and ask how well, or not, they were met. In both cases, we only get a narrow perspective on the activity as a whole. Reflective practice, on the other hand, can enable us to see the depths and richness of what has been created and accomplished, however small or seemingly insignificant. Not only is reflection of benefit to our families, community, churches and colleagues, but it can also bring great meaning for ourselves.

Considering the range of potential benefits working in this way can have, Canavan, Pinkerton and Dolan believe that reflective practice should be core to family support practice and not an optional, 'nice-to-do' extra. They recognise that 'how workers do what they do is of equal importance to what they do'.[115] Although they're writing in relation to secular support, the same principles apply in ministry. Time should be spent analysing both what took place and also how to gain a greater understanding of what's taking place. Incorporating this into our day-to-day work accumulates our knowledge and understanding, developing our ability to become ongoing reflective practitioners.

Becoming a reflective practitioner

Bearing in mind the breadth of ways reflective practice may benefit our work and ministry, what does it look like? How do we go about incorporating it into our working patterns and life? There are two primary ways in which this happens, according to Donald Schon: reflection-in-action and reflection-on-action.[116]

Reflection-in-action takes place during an activity: as a group or session is taking place, we're observing what's going on. We might, for example, notice that in the toddler group a few parents aren't engaging much with other parents; they seem to be on the fringes of activity all the time and reluctant to join in conversations. Reflection-in-action also enables us to think of reasons why this is and some possible ways to address the issue. As Schon states, 'Reflection-in-action is where we may reflect in the midst of action without interrupting it. Our thinking serves to reshape what we're doing while we are doing it.'[117]

It may not be instinctive to some of us to work in this way. We may find we're so deeply involved in the delivery of an activity or the organisation of a session itself that we barely have time to look around. But it can be helpful to stop, even just for a few moments, and see what strikes us, aiming to take one thing away to analyse later on.

Reflection-on-action takes place after an activity has been completed. We are probably more familiar with this type of reflection. For instance, once a holiday club has come to an end we spend time considering what went well, what was a struggle and what we'd like to do differently next time. This form of reflection can require thinking more deeply about what went on, considering our own values and responses and the place these had in what unfolded. It may be a more instinctive form of reflection, but it is equally easy to overlook as we move on to other priorities. Bassot states that one of the benefits 'is that it can prevent your practice from routine stagnation, by encouraging you to turn off your "automatic pilot".'[118]

Reflection in both of these instances is influenced by a range of factors – who was involved, how the activity unfolded and when it took place. There is also our personal circumstances, mood and attitude at the time to consider, which we may be tempted to either overlook or focus too much on. Trying to strike an objective balance is key. Returning to what took place and applying critical and analytical skills as we reflect can provide valuable insight that influences our practice into the future.

Features of reflective practice

There are some primary features of reflective practice worth considering. These essential principles inform us that experience leads to reflection, which leads to learning, which then shapes our experience. In other words, as we grapple with ways to deal with a situation, our understanding of it grows and this learning leads us to make adjustments or introduce new things. It is an ongoing cycle that enables us to unpack how and why certain outcomes happened.

Reflection isn't done for the sake of it – without consequences; it compels us to move forwards, adapting our approaches as we go. Reflection brings about change. This makes it very much an active process that goes deeper than scratching at the surface of what took place. It requires us to intentionally consider what may be the cause of certain events or outcomes. It seeks out the issues and fine-tunes our problem-solving skills, recognising that this is a usual experience in ministry – there will always be dilemmas to face and respond to. By acknowledging this as an inevitable part of our work we can become better equipped to handle the challenges that come our way.

Reflection invites us to look at our work from a variety of perspectives, urging us to include viewpoints other than our own to inform our under-standing of what took place. It requires scrutiny of the views we hold and assumptions we make, in order for our reflection to be more fully rounded. This all forms part of the cyclical nature of reflective practice. As we progress through ministry, we recognise the flow that reflection takes from experience through to learning – all of which enable us to become better at planning our work into the future.

There are a range of theories and models of reflection that seek to clarify the process and break it down into discrete stages. Graham Gibbs' reflective cycle[119] includes six phases (see figure opposite). In this process, time is given not only to reflect on the events and experience of what happened but also to our emotional response to it. We identify what occurred but also how it made us feel. We then move on to consider the positives and negatives of the situation by evaluating these observations before analysing them in greater detail. These stages of the process aid us in helping make sense of what took place and why certain issues arose or particular difficulties were encountered. As we then reach conclusions, asking ourselves if there were other actions or interventions we could have made, we begin forming an action plan. This plan, which includes key points for next time, brings us back to the beginning of the cycle and gives an opportunity to apply our learning at the next occasion.

Gibbs' reflective cycle

A key phase here is the need to analyse, and not simply describe, what happened. Analysis is where we break down the situation into smaller parts, exploring events in greater depth and asking significant questions, striving to do this with objectivity as far as is possible. This requires a degree of detachment, which might be difficult as we can be personally heavily invested in the work we do. The churches where we serve may also be our worshipping homes, and we may have deep and long-established relationships with people that colour our view and ability to judge objectively. Yet if we ignore this vital analytical stage, our reflective practice will be much weaker for it and we risk our learning being insufficient when applied to future activities.

There will undoubtedly be reservations when it comes to reflecting on our practice. The barriers are numerous, but it's good to name them and actively ask ourselves why we may be finding it difficult to overcome them. Take a look at this short list. You may want to consider which is the most significant stumbling block for you.

- *Time* – Our workload and ministry responsibility is so vast that we have little time to dedicate to reflecting during or after. The daily demands mean we're often exhausted, finding it difficult to manage all the various aspects of our role and personal lives combined.

- *Other people* – The wide range of stakeholders and interested parties involved in ministry, such as volunteers, church leaders, the congregation and the families themselves, means there are too many other opinions that can confuse and sway us.

- *Ourselves* – Our own characters may hinder us in pursuing a more intentionally reflective approach. We may be self-critical and lean towards always seeing the faults in what we do or, at the other extreme, take for granted how our work occurs and don't see the need to look any more deeply into how and why we work the way we do.

- *No better way* – Maybe we lack a willingness to entertain the idea that there could be a different way. Once we have spent years building experience and shaping our ministry, there's a strong possibility we have grown reluctant to explore the alternatives: to consider there might be a different or better way. Reflective practice requires us to work on our ability to remain open-minded and willing to move out of our comfort zone to test out new ideas.

Having read this list, you may want to ignore it and carry on reading, but I encourage you to pause and return to it again. Ask yourself whether they're legitimate concerns or rather excuses you've presented. Be prepared to be honest with yourself. Everyone has a blind spot – something about themselves they're unaware of – so you may want to have a conversation with a trusted friend or colleague and mull this over for a longer period. Embracing becoming a reflective practitioner may make us fearful of what we'll uncover – about ourselves primarily, but also about how we choose to undertake our work. Choosing to take small steps in that direction can grow confidence and allay those fears, especially if we do it prayerfully in partnership with God, knowing he loves and equips us for the task in hand.

Reflective practice methods

Identifying your preferences when becoming a reflective practitioner may take a while. There are a range of tools available to us, which we can test to see whether they are compatible with our individual approaches and work settings. We'll explore three of them: the reflective journal, peer support and mentoring.

Reflective journal

This may be a familiar tool, which we might have heard referred to as a learning journal. It's a place to record observations and feelings we've experienced; to help us organise our thoughts and ideas, fine-tuning them in the process; and to respond to any questions that arise as a result. A journal offers an opportunity to articulate our ministry experiences as we write down the various aspects during our reflection process. It's a tool for critical evaluation that raises awareness of our own behaviours and the strategies we employ. Being reflective through the written word can encourage us to develop our own voice as we wrestle with any difficulties encountered or accomplishments made. Of course, our reflections are not restricted to the written word; journalling can incorporate illustrations and other motifs that represent our responses. It is highly individual and can be structured in ways that reflect our character and preferences. The journal may include further questions we intend to follow up or additional conversations to go away and have. The scope is broad, and its usefulness for informing the ongoing development of our ministry depends very much on us.

Journal tips
- Keep a rhythm to when you write: daily or weekly.
- Know you're writing for yourself; it's not going to be assessed, so don't think of it as an essay.
- Keep it informal, use your own language and write in the first person.
- Find a relaxing and comfortable spot to journal in.
- Type, write or sketch – whatever is most beneficial for you.
- Make a note of the 'what' and sequence of events, but also look back on the process as a whole.
- Note any questions that arise, pinpointing aspects for future follow-up.
- Make connections between your experience and theories and theology.

A reflective journal is intended to be our personal record of our work and ministry. As we commit to the process of keeping it, it's worth thinking through what we hope to achieve and what the long-term goals are that we have for our practice. Our ability to reflect and draw conclusions from our practice steadily grows as we integrate the writing into our regular flow of work. The journal will become a valuable record of our work development, and flicking back through its pages will remind us of progress made. Sometimes ministry developments can feel insignificant; a journal is a powerful tool for demonstrating the direction of travel and achievements made along the way.

Peer support

There's a reason why we often feel the urge to gather with others to discuss and share about what we do. Whether it's at training events, conferences or catch-ups over coffee, we seem to instinctively know that getting together with others involved in similar work to ourselves is beneficial. It gives us those 'me too!' moments, when we identify similar issues or concerns, and provides much-needed encouragement and support when we may be feeling isolated or challenged.

Peer groups or communities of practice offer spaces to meet with other practitioners and engage in meaningful times of critical reflection on the work we're doing. Bassot highlights the dangers of not pursuing reflective practice as a collaborative activity: 'We can become immersed in our own point of view, seeing things only from our perspective, which is inevitably narrow, limited and even biased.'[120] There is a place for our individual reflection but also a powerful case to be part of a collective, reflecting with others in the same field, as this can prove enormously fruitful. Groups provide constructive contexts to discuss and share experiences and ideas and to offer support. There needs to be a balance of listening and responding, so participants know they can be heard. These may often be organised on a geographical basis, taking into account the travel necessary to get together. They offer a space to locate our own critical thinking within wider frameworks of how others reflect on similar ministry experiences.

Peer support tips
- Meet regularly at a frequency that suits the group.
- Decide a helpful number of members – five to eight is often a good size.
- Agree your own agenda.

- Discuss and agree a framework for the times you meet, establishing the parameters for conversations at a level of formality that works for the group.
- Respect the views of others and give them ample time to share.
- Be aware of others' feelings and own them, especially strong ones.
- Make prayer a feature of your time together.

Mentoring

Mentoring is a way 'to support and encourage people to manage their own learning in order that they may maximise their potential, develop their skills, improve their performance and become the person they want to be'.[121] Mentoring relationships are helpful within reflective practice, as they provide spaces for dialogue that can deepen thinking and give opportunities for questions to be raised that might not have otherwise been considered. Through developing and investing in this relationship our confidence as practitioners can grow and our eyes be opened to alternative ways of fostering ministry practice.

For some practitioners, there may be elements of mentoring within one-to-one line management, but it can be valuable to find someone to meet with independently to reflect on our work experiences. Who this is is a matter of personal preference; it could be someone with experience in a similar role or someone in another faith or church context. It is worth spending time identifying someone we feel able to build trust and develop a mentoring relationship with, someone able to be a 'critical friend' – that is, not someone who dishes out criticism (in a harsh, judgemental fashion) but someone able to offer critique, help assess and discuss with us ways to change or improve into the future. Canavan, Pinkerton and Dolan state that 'mutual goal-setting for supervision and reflective practice can be helpful to both the manager and frontline worker alike'.[122] This includes asking questions, such as: what is urgent and immediate that has to be addressed swiftly? What are the medium-term issues for consideration, and what are the longer-term goals that will drive ministry forward?

Mentoring tips
- Establish the parameters for the mentoring relationship.
- Agree to meet at a mutually convenient time and commit to doing so on a regular basis.
- Keep the session to between 30 and 75 minutes.

- Recognise that mentoring is a journey for the mentee and mentor and that results happen over time.
- Explore questions relevant to practice and related to experiences, both in the short and longer term.

These are an introductory selection of possible routes into becoming a reflective practitioner. We may find ourselves drawn to particular ones over others. Whatever we choose, it's important that they work for us and that we consider using a combination of different tools, as they can be useful for different purposes.

Conclusion

This chapter has sought to highlight the importance of reflective practice in family ministry. Alongside planning and preparation, reflective practice provides a solid foundation for evaluating the effectiveness of our work, an alternative to simply watching attendance levels. Ministry with families is often demanding, requiring a high level of commitment from practitioners, who need to employ a range of skills in a range of circumstances. It's rarely straightforward! By developing ourselves as reflective practitioners we can grow our resilience and ability to respond to the most challenging of situations.

There are elements of mindfulness in being reflective. To become a reflective practitioner requires paying attention to what is going on during our work: to recognise the paradigms we're working within and how they impact on who we are and what we do. Reflecting on our practice helps us to engage with alternative perspectives and explore other possibilities; it nurtures in us a desire to grow and learn; it enables us to recognise both the positive and the more challenging aspects of ministry. We think more deeply.

Becoming a reflective practitioner requires us to commit to an ongoing dialogue as we consider experiences, analyse and evaluate them, then form conclusions which will influence our future action. With the help of others around us, offering friendship, support and a critical eye, we can deepen and enrich our ministry in a raft of unanticipated ways.

All of this will hugely benefit the families we're working with. As Canavan, Pinkerton and Dolan reiterate, being reflective helps practitioners 'to be confident that what they are doing has meaning and significance for improving the lives of those they seek to support'.

Ultimately, reflective practice can transform us. It can build our confidence and expertise, improve our well-being and help us as we manage complex roles and responsibilities. Over time we will be able to look back and have a much stronger sense of all that's been accomplished through embracing our identity as reflective practitioners.

Questions for reflection

- Imagine a continuum from unreflective to very critically reflective. Where would you currently place yourself? How much of a priority is it for you to be reflective?

- What may be some of the barriers you face to becoming a more reflective practitioner?

- Are you aware of any peer groups or communities of practice that meet in your area? How could you become involved?

- Who do you know who could provide you with some mentoring support? Why might they be a good person for this?

FINAL THOUGHTS

What a long way we've come! Through these pages we've explored the current context for family ministry in the UK, recognising the diversity of forms of family that now exist. Parents, carers, children and young people, along with their extended families and friends, are working out what it means to be family with and for each other in a host of different ways. Family remains important. What it looks like and how it happens in households continues to change. For our ministry to continue to be relevant and authentic we need to remain connected to what's happening in communities around us. Only by doing so can we ensure that the ministry we offer will be meeting the needs of those in our churches and neighbourhoods. There's a danger that if we continue to harbour ideas of families as they were, or perceptions of what they ought to be, we'll find our work to be increasingly irrelevant. If we want to offer the kinds of support and care families are looking for, we need to start with them. Building relationships is one of the key tasks in ministry. Forming these might not always be straightforward – some of them will be downright challenging and difficult – but it ensures that we generate activities they feel able to participate in and communities they have a genuine sense of belonging to.

As family ministry practitioners, our role is essential. How we approach ministry and the way we set strategic goals, allocate resources and collaborate with colleagues will shape our ministry with families. These areas have been highlighted here to help us develop a dynamic and significant ministry with those we're engaging with. By shifting from being reactive towards being proactive, it's possible to cultivate work that effectively meets the needs of families and intentionally grows community. By shifting our focus to exploring how we can better support families as they function together, rather than emphasising the form they take, we can help all households to thrive. We need to adopt practices that focus on families' strengths, nurturing these so that the contemporary narrative of families as broken and dysfunctional is transformed to one of hopefulness and vitality – and one that sees practitioners as having a key role in communicating joy and optimism in one of the cornerstones of societal life.

Be creative and innovative, embracing an attitude of giving something a go without fear of it failing. If it does (it often does!), it provides an opportunity for learning before we head on to the next challenge. Family ministry requires courage and determination. When we find ourselves entering uncharted territory, we need to summon these in bucketloads. Embrace an approach to ministry that intertwines mission and support, which doesn't silo the spiritual yearnings people have. We need spaces where families can be their whole selves, in the mess and grit of all the struggles they encounter in life, receiving practical and prayerful support when things are difficult. Recognise that all of us walk our own roads of faith, travelling at differing paces under the attentive eye of our generous and loving God. Underestimate your influence at your own peril. Sharpen your focus. Be a taker of the good news of Christ into all the settings you find yourself in: schools, toddler groups, planning meetings, holiday clubs, all-age services, supermarkets, prayer times, conversations in coffee shops. Whether they are secular or faith spaces, shine brightly in the knowledge that God equips and empowers you for this task. Ask often for him to provide what you need – energy, encouragement, supporters, grace, patience, love – knowing that he walks alongside you as you seek to blur the edges between church, faith, community and the world.

Let these final words be ones of exhortation for you, from Paul as he ends his letter to the Ephesians:

> Therefore, put on every piece of God's armour so you will be able to resist the enemy in the time of evil. Then after the battle you will be standing firm. Stand your ground, putting on the belt of truth and the body armour of God's righteousness. For shoes, put on the peace that comes from the Good News so that you will be fully prepared. In addition to all of these, hold up the shield of faith to stop the fiery arrows of the devil. Put on salvation as your helmet, and take the sword of the Spirit, which is the word of God. Pray in the Spirit at all times and on every occasion. Stay alert and be persistent in your prayers for all believers everywhere.
>
> EPHESIANS 6:13–18

Go forth, be a blessing and be blessed.

FURTHER READING AND OTHER RESOURCES

1 The changing shape of family

Jack Balswick and Judith Balswick, *The Family: A Christian perspective on the contemporary home* (Baker Academic, 2014) – brings together contemporary family life, research insights and biblical truth.

Deborah Chambers, *A Sociology of Family Life: Change and diversity in intimate relations* (Polity, 2012) – explores the growing diversity of family life.

Fiona Williams, *Rethinking Families* (Calouste Gulbenkian Foundation, 2005) – sets out the main trends in family life with reference to research and the impact on people's lives.

2 Theology for family ministry

Michael Anthony and Michelle Anthony, *A Theology for Family Ministries* (B&H, 2011) – draws together theology on a range of family perspectives.

Carol J. Gallagher, *Family Theology: Finding God in very human relationships* (Morehouse, 2012) – features both personal and traditional stories of faith, complemented by contemporary insights.

David E. Garland and Diana R. Garland, *Flawed Families of the Bible: How God's grace works through imperfect relationships* (Brazos, 2007) – what does the Bible have to say about families? Explores the pain and promise of family life.

Adrian Thatcher, *Theology and Families* (Blackwell, 2007) – useful for exploring theology in the context of practical discussions about families and children.

Building Faith (**buildfaith.org**) – provides resources and articles to inspire faith development in a range of settings.

3 Family ministry today

Ivy Beckwith, *Postmodern Children's Ministry: Ministry to children in the 21st century* (Zondervan, 2004) – a vision for children's ministry that sustains their faith and offers ideas to keep them engaged.

Consultative Group on Ministry among Children (CGMC), *Core Skills for Family Ministry: Developing key skills for church-based family ministry* (BRF, 2015) – foundation-training and equipping for those engaged in family ministry.

The Methodist Church/Children's Ministry Network, *We Are Family: The Changing landscape of family ministry* (2014) – research exploring the nature of contemporary family ministry in the UK.

Paul Renfro, Brandon Shields and Jay Strother, *Perspectives on Family Ministry: 3 views* (B&H, 2009) – explores churches' approaches to family ministry.

Cliff College Certificate in Family Ministry (**cliffcollege.ac.uk/students/ shortcourses/cliff-certificates/cifm**) – a week-long course designed for family work practitioners within the church and the community, run in partnership with the Methodist Learning Network and BRF.

Coram Family and Childcare (**familyandchildcaretrust.org**) – charity working to make the UK a better place for families with a focus on childcare and the early years.

CURBS (**curbsproject.org.uk**) – Christian charity set up in response to the need for resources and training for church-based workers in inner cities and on outer urban estates.

D6 (**d6family.com**) – a US family ministry movement connecting church and home. Resources and curriculum for both.

Gingerbread (**gingerbread.org.uk**) – charity supporting single parent families to live secure, happy and fulfilling lives.

Home for Good (**homeforgood.org.uk**) – charity dedicated to finding a home for every child who needs one, growing a network of people, churches and local movements across the UK.

Messy Church (**messychurch.org.uk**) – creating new spaces of faith for people of all ages.

Working Families (**workingfamilies.org.uk**) – the UK's work-life balance charity.

Youth and Childrens Work magazine (**youthandchildrens.work**) – contains articles on current family ministry topics.

4 Be strategic

Diana Garland, *Family Ministry: A comprehensive guide* (IVP, 2012) – draws together her extensive research, understanding of family and approaches to ministry in one book.

Timothy Paul Jones and John David Trentham, *Practical Family Ministry: A collection of ideas for your church*, (Randall House, 2015) – offers practical strategies for family ministry that forges links between church and home.

Megan Marshman and Michelle Anthony, *7 Family Ministry Essentials: A strategy for culture change in children's and student ministries* (David C. Cook, 2015) – the guiding essentials that equip practitioners in ministry with families.

5 Be supportive

John Canavan, John Pinkerton and Pat Dolan, *Understanding Family Support: Policy, practice and theory* (Jessica Kingsley, 2016) – as the subtitle says, brings together policy, practice and theory.

Caroline Dollard, *Seeking God Together: A Companion for parish communities in meeting, welcoming and accompanying families* (House on Rock, 2018) – guidance on ways to support families pastorally throughout the various seasons of life.

Nick Frost, Shaheen Abbott and Tracey Race, *Family Support: Prevention, early intervention and early help* (Polity, 2015) – explores the contemporary debate and thinking around family support as well as practical approaches.

Emma Sawyer and Sheryl Burton, *A Practical Guide to Early Intervention and Family Support: Assessing needs and building resilience in families affected by parental mental health problems or substance misuse* (Jessica Kingsley, 2012) – ways to offer effective family support including pointers, models, tool and practice examples.

1277 (**1277.org.uk**) – national network of church-based toddler groups.

Action for Children (**actionforchildren.org.uk**) – charity aiming to protect and support children and young people, providing practical and emotional care and support, ensuring their voices are heard, and campaigning to bring lasting improvements to their lives.

Additional Needs Alliance (**additionalneedsalliance.org.uk**) – charity helping churches to include, support, create places of belonging for and spiritually grow children, young people and young adults with additional needs or disabilities.

Care for the Family (**cff.org.uk**) – national charity that aims to promote strong family life and to help those who face family difficulties.

Family Action (**family-action.org.uk**) – charity dedicated to building stronger families.

Kids Matter (**kidsmatter.org.uk**) – delivering parenting programmes to those in disadvantaged communities.

Playtime (**careforthefamily.org.uk/faith-in-the-family/playtime**) – provides support and advice for anyone interested in engaging with young families in a toddler group setting.

Transforming Lives for Good (**tlg.org.uk**) – charity helping churches to bring hope and a future to struggling children and their families through a range of initiatives.

Who Let The Dads Out? (**wholetthedadsout.org.uk**) – part of Care for the Family; resources churches to effectively engage with dads, father figures and their children, primarily through parent-and-child groups.

6 Be collaborative

Robert Crosby, *The Teaming Church: Ministry in the age of collaboration* (Abingdon, 2012) – provides biblical motivations, examples and practical approaches for creating a team culture in church.

The Children's Society (**childrenssociety.org.uk**) – a charity that works with the country's most vulnerable children and young people.

Early Years Alliance (**eyalliance.org.uk**) – a charity seeking to influence early years policy and practice, offering information, advice and training.

NCVO (**ncvo.org.uk**) – a charity championing the voluntary sector and volunteering, doing this by connecting, representing and supporting voluntary organisations.

National Society for Prevention of Cruelty to Children (**nspcc.org.uk**) – a charity seeking to protect children and fighting to end child abuse.

Sure Start Children's Centres – provide family support in local communities. Find your local centre at **gov.uk/find-sure-start-childrens-centre**.

7 Be intergenerational

Kathie Amidei, Jim Merhaut and John Roberto, *Generations Together: Caring, praying, learning, celebrating and serving faithfully* (Lifelong Faith, 2014) – presents a vision for how faith can be cultivated across the generations.

Eleanor Bird, *Blended: A call to reimagine our church family – rethinking how we can be church together* (BRF, 2015) – explores ways to bring the church together in worship and learning.

Holly Catterton Allen, *InterGenerate: Transforming churches through intergenerational ministry* (ACU, 2018) – various perspectives on generational theory, fresh biblical and theological insights and practical steps for ministry.

Holly Catterton Allen and Christine Lawton Ross, *Intergenerational Christian Formation: Bringing the whole church together in ministry, community and worship* (IVP Academic, 2012) – offers a complete framework for intentional Christian formation across the generations.

Mathew Deprez, *Join Generations: Becoming unashamedly intergenerational* (AtlantiCreative, 2013) – a call to bring the generations together for the faith development of all.

Jason Gardner, *Mend the Gap: Can the church reconnect the generations?* (IVP, 2008) – seeks to inspire us to reconnect the generations.

Kara Powell, Brad Griffin and Chap Clark, *Sticky Faith* (Zondervan, 2011) - combines research and the authors' own experience to empower parents to nurture faith that lasts.

Peter Menconi, *The Intergenerational Church: Understanding congregations from WWII to www.com* (MT Sage, 2010) – a practical book to equip the differing generations in the church to worship, learn and go on mission together.

Martyn Payne, *Messy Togetherness: Being intergenerational in Messy Church* (BRF, 2016) – explores how Messy Church as an all-age expression of church brings benefits of this to the wider church community.

Engage Worship (**engageworship.org**) – resources for all-age services that enable generations to gather and experience creative, meaningful worship together.

Explore Together (**content.scriptureunion.org.uk/explore-together**) – all-age worship resources from Scripture Union that enables everyone to learn together.

Roots (**rootsontheweb.com**) – publishes lectionary-based resources for adults, children, young people and all ages together, including family faith material.

Sticky Faith (**stickyfaith.org**) – strategic approach helping to develop faith in families that lasts a lifetime. Part of Fuller Youth Institute (**fulleryouthinstitute.org**).

8 Be missional

Chap Clark and Kara Powell, *Deep Justice in a Broken World: Helping your kids serve others and right the wrongs around them* (Zondervan, 2008) – makes the case for young people's engagement in transformative social justice.

Steven Emery-Wright and Ed Mackenzie, *Networks for Faith Formation: Relational bonds and the spiritual growth of youth* (Wipf and Stock, 2017) – explores the wider set of relationships needed to help faith grow for children and young people. Contains a chapter specifically on mission.

9 Be holy at home

Reggie Joiner, *Think Orange* (David C. Cook, 2009) – explores how the church and families can work together for the benefit of children and young people.

Timothy Paul Jones, *Family Ministry Field Guide: How the church can equip parents to make disciples* (Wesleyan, 2011) – offers a practical plan to equip parents to be the primary faith influencers in their children's lives, moving beyond mere programming into genuine spiritual transformation.

Leif Kehrwald, John Roberto, Gene Roehlkepartain and Jolene Roehl-kepartain, *Families at the Center of Faith Formation* (Hillspring, 2016) – calls for a new approach to faith formation centred on families.

Steve Legg and Bekah Legg, *All Together: The family devotional book* (CWR, 2017) – devotional readings for families to spend time learning from the Bible, and growing closer together.

Ed Mackenzie and Gareth Crispin, *Together With God: An introduction to family worship* (Morse-Brown, 2016) – book and podcast, resources and conversations on faith, family and the church today.

Kara Powell and Steven Argue, *Growing With: Every parent's guide to helping teenagers and young adults thrive in their faith, family and future* (Baker Books, 2019) – a parent's guide to raising teenagers and young adults.

Rachel Turner, *Parenting Children for a Life of Faith: Helping children meet and know God* (omnibus edition, BRF, 2018) – explores how parents can fulfil their potential at home as they raise children to know God and grow in faith.

Jonathan Williams, *Gospel Family: Cultivating family discipleship, family worship and family missions* (Lucid Books, 2015) – seeks to cultivate family discipleship, worship and mission.

GodVenture (**godventure.co.uk**) – resources for families to use to grow in faith together.

Homefront magazine (**homefrontmag.com**) – equips parents to create fun, spiritually forming times in their homes.

Kitchen Table Project (**kitchentable.org.uk**) – inspiration and resources for parents and carers to bring matters of faith into their every lives with children.

Little Worship Company (**littleworshipcompany.com**) – resources for churches, playgroups and families to nurture faith and worship.

Parenting For Faith (**parentingforfaith.org**) – resources for parents and carers to equip them as they nurture faith at home.

10 Be reflective

Barbara Bassot, *The Reflective Practice Guide: An interdisciplinary approach to critical reflection* (Routledge, 2015) – a source of support, guidance and inspiration for all those who want to think about practice at a deeper level, question approaches, challenge assumptions and gain greater self-awareness.

Eric Parsloe and Melville Leedham, *Coaching and Mentoring: Practical conversations to improve learning* (Kogan Page, 2009) – creating conversations that aid personal development.

The Well Learning Hub – Methodist Church network for children, youth and family workers. Go to **methodist.org.uk/our-work/children-youth-family-ministry** and follow the links. See also its Facebook page and Youtube channel.

NOTES

1 Diana R. Garland, *Family Ministry: A comprehensive guide*, 2nd edition (IVP Academic, 2012), p. 43.
2 Stephen R. Covey, *The 7 Habits of Highly Effective People* (Simon and Schuster, 1989).
3 As Deborah Chambers highlights, 'sociological accounts of family and personal relationships in the nineteenth and early twentieth centuries were characterised by anxieties about the decline of traditional family values'. Deborah Chambers, *A Sociology of Family Life: Change and diversity in intimate relations* (Polity, 2012), p. 14.
4 Chambers, *A Sociology of Family Life*, p. 20.
5 Garland, *Family Ministry*, p. 29.
6 Fiona Williams, *Rethinking Families* (Calouste Gulbenkian Foundation, 2005), p. 15.
7 Garland, *Family Ministry*, p. 294.
8 Williams, *Rethinking Families*, p. 17.
9 *We Are Family: The changing face of family ministry*, research report (The Methodist Church, 2014), **methodist.org.uk/media/3291/final_waf_a4_research_findings.pdf**; the updated 2017 report is available at **methodist.org.uk/media/3292/we-are-family-booklet-1017.pdf**.
10 Williams, *Rethinking Families*, p. 18.
11 Williams, *Rethinking Families*, p. 6.
12 Chambers, *A Sociology of Family Life*, p. 41.
13 Chambers, *A Sociology of Family Life*, p. 8.
14 See Williams, *Rethinking Families*.
15 Williams, *Rethinking Families*, p. 55.
16 Office for National Statistics, 'Female employment rate (aged 16 to 64, seasonally adjusted), **ons.gov.uk/employmentandlabourmarket/peopleinwork/employmentandemployeetypes/timeseries/lf25/lms**
17 Working Families and Bright Horizons Family Solutions, *Modern Families Index 2017*, **workingfamilies.org.uk/wp-content/uploads/2017/01/MFI_2017_Report_UK_FINAL_web-1.pdf**, p. 2.
18 Jessica Woodroffe, *Not Having It All: How motherhood reduces women's pay and employment prospects* (Fawcett Society, 2009), p. 3.
19 Quoted in Chambers, *A Sociology of Family Life*, p. 21.

20 Chambers, *A Sociology of Family Life*, p. 56.
21 Williams, *Rethinking Families*, p. 24.
22 Quoted in Williams, *Rethinking Families*, p. 17.
23 Williams, *Rethinking Families*, p. 17.
24 Williams, *Rethinking Families*, p. 8.
25 Office for National Statistics (ONS), 'Families and Households: 2015', 5 November 2015, **ons.gov.uk/peoplepopulationandcommunity/ birthsdeathsandmarriages/families/bulletins/ familiesandhouseholds/2015-11-05**.
26 ONS, 'Families and Households: 2015'.
27 Taylor Tepper, 'The surprising reason you should live near your parents', 23 February 2017, **time.com/money/4670440/layoff-millennial-families-live-near-home**.
28 Williams, *Rethinking Families*, p. 26.
29 Adrian Thatcher, *Theology and Families* (Blackwell, 2007), p. 3.
30 Jack O. Balswick and Judith K. Balswick, *The Family* (Baker Academic, 2014), p. 3.
31 Garland, *Family Ministry*, ch. 3.
32 Thatcher, *Theology and Families*, p. 20.
33 Garland, *Family Ministry*, p. 88 – referencing Matthew 13:47.
34 David E. Garland and Diana R. Garland, *Flawed Families of the Bible* (Brazos Press, 2007), p. 11.
35 Leon M. Blanchette Jr, 'Spiritual markers in the life of a child', in Michael Anthony and Michelle Anthony (eds), *A Theology for Family Ministries* (B&H Academic, 2011), p. 127.
36 Garland, *Family Ministry*, p. 444.
37 The Methodist Church, *Holiness and Justice*, **methodist.org.uk/media/3137/ conf-holiness-and-justice-booklet-0716.pdf**.
38 Steven Emery-Wright and Ed Mackenzie, *Networks for Faith Formation* (Wipf and Stock, 2017), p. 43.
39 John Wesley, 'The preface' in John Wesley and Charles Wesley, *Hymns and Sacred Poems* (1743).
40 Andrew Stobart, 'Editorial', *Holiness: The journal of Wesley House Cambridge* 2 (2016), pp. 279–80, **wesley.cam.ac.uk/wp-content/uploads/2014/09/01-editorial.pdf**.
41 Quoted in Thatcher, *Theology and Families*, p. 81.
42 Thatcher, *Theology and Families*, p. 47
43 Balswick and Balswick, *The Family*, p. 2.
44 Daniel L. Migliore, *Faith Seeking Understanding* (W. B. Eerdmans, 2004), p. 76.
45 Balswick and Balswick, *The Family*, p. 20.
46 Emery-Wright and Mackenzie, *Networks for Faith Formation*, p. 8.
47 Balswick and Balswick, *The Family*, p. 322.
48 Thatcher, *Theology and Families*, p. 49.
49 Richard Melick Jr, 'New Testament teachings on the family' in Anthony and

Anthony (eds), *A Theology for Family Ministries*, p. 98.

50 Thatcher, *Theology and Families*, p. 52.

51 Thatcher, *Theology and Families*, p. 52.

52 *We Are Family*, p. 9.

53 Garland, *Family Ministry*, p. 113.

54 Timothy Paul Jones, 'Foundations for family ministry', in T.P. Jones (ed.), *Perspectives on Family Ministry: Three views* (B&H Academic, 2009), p. 40.

55 Timothy Paul Jones and Randy Stinson, 'Family ministry models', in Anthony and Anthony (eds), *A Theology for Family Ministries*, p. 173.

56 This quote is from a website that is no longer live. Mark DeVries is president and founder of Ministry Architects: **ministryarchitects.com**.

57 *We Are Family*, p. 11.

58 *We Are Family*, p. 12.

59 *We Are Family*, p. 10.

60 Going for Growth, 'The Toddler Project research findings', p. 7, available to download from **going4growth.com/index.php/growth_in_faith_and_worship/early_years**.

61 *We Are Family*, p. 42.

62 Angela Anning and Mog Ball, *Improving Services for Young Children* (Sage, 2008), p. 12.

63 *We Are Family*, p. 17.

64 Leif Kehrwald, John Roberto, Gene Roehlkepartain and Jolene Roehlkepartain, *Families at the Center of Faith Formation* (Lifelong Faith, 2016), p. 153.

65 Garland, *Family Ministry*, p. 484.

66 Timothy Paul Jones, *The Family Ministry Field Guide* (Wesleyan, 2011).

67 Garland, *Family Ministry*, p. 489.

68 Garland, *Family Ministry*, p. 449.

69 John Canavan, John Pinkerton and Pat Dolan, *Understanding Family Support* (Jessica Kingsley, 2016) p. 20.

70 Garland, *Family Ministry*, p. 489.

71 Emma Sawyer and Sheryl Burton, *A Practical Guide to Early Intervention and Family Support* (Jessica Kingsley, 2009), p. 142.

72 Garland, *Family Ministry*, p. 491.

73 Canavan et al., *Understanding Family Support*, p. 83.

74 Garland, *Family Ministry*, p. 555.

75 Garland, *Family Ministry*, p. 484.

76 Robert C. Crosby, *The Teaming Church: Ministry in the age of collaboration* (Abingdon Press, 2012), p. 12.

77 Eleanor Bird, *Blended* (BRF, 2015).

78 Emery-Wright and Mackenzie, *Networks for Faith Formation*, p. 24.

79 Peter N. Stearns, 'Historical trends in intergenerational contacts', *Journal of Children in Contemporary Society*, 20:3–4, 1989, p. 30.

80 Peter Menconi, *The Intergenerational Church* (Sage, 2010), p. 28.

81 John Roberto, 'Reimagining family faith formation: families at the center' in Kehrwald et al., *Families at the Center of Faith Formation*, p. 70.

82 Church Growth Research Programme, quoted in Emery-Wright and Mackenzie, *Networks for Faith Formation*, p. 33.

83 Emery-Wright and Mackenzie, *Networks for Faith Formation*, p. 108.

84 Holly Catterton Allen and Christine Lawton Ross, *Intergenerational Christian Formation* (IVP, 2012), p. 42.

85 Joseph Rhea, 'Why the church needs intergenerational friendships', 8 January 2015, **thegospelcoalition.org/article/why-the-church-needs-intergenerational-friendships**.

86 Menconi, *The Intergenerational Church*, p. 201.

87 Martyn Payne, *Messy Togetherness: Being intergenerational in Messy Church* (BRF, 2016).

88 Allen and Ross, *Intergenerational Christian Formation*, p. 84.

89 Menconi, *The Intergenerational Church*.

90 Emery-Wright and Mackenzie, *Networks for Faith Formation*, p. 100.

91 Bird, *Blended*.

92 There's a more detailed exploration of these ideas in chapter 14 of Allen and Ross, *Intergenerational Christian Formation*.

93 Allen and Ross, *Intergenerational Christian Formation*; Kathie Amidei, Jim Merhaut and John Roberto, *Generations Together* (Lifelong Faith, 2014), ch. 5.

94 Allen and Ross, *Intergenerational Christian Formation*, p. 63.

95 Emery-Wright and Mackenzie, *Networks for Faith Formation*, p. 95.

96 Emery-Wright and Mackenzie, *Networks for Faith Formation*, p. 97.

97 Emery-Wright and Mackenzie, *Networks for Faith Formation*, p. 98.

98 Scott Douglas, 'Family on mission' in Timothy Paul Jones and John David Trentham (eds), *Practical Family Ministry* (Randall House, 2015), p. 60.

99 Douglas, 'Family on mission', p. 62.

100 Jonathan Williams, *Gospel Family* (Lucid Books, 2015), p. 167.

101 Douglas, 'Family on mission', p. 64.

102 Emery-Wright and Mackenzie, *Networks for Faith Formation*, p. 103.

103 Emery-Wright and Mackenzie, *Networks for Faith Formation*, p. 102.

104 Ivy Beckwith, *Postmodern Children's Ministry* (Zondervan, 2004), p. 68.

105 Ed Mackenzie and Gareth Crispin, *Together with God: An introduction to family worship* (Morse-Brown Publishing, 2016), p. 5.

106 Garland, *Family Ministry*, p. 413.

107 Rick Rusaw and Eric Swanson, *The Externally Focused Church* (Group, 2004), pp. 88–89.

108 Reggie Joiner, *Think Orange* (David C Cook Publishing, 2009).

109 Beckwith, *Postmodern Children's Ministry*, p. 119.

110 Rachel Turner, *Parenting Children for a Life of Faith* (BRF, 2010). This is now available in an omnibus edition (BRF, 2018), which includes her two other titles in the series (*Parenting Children for a Life of Purpose* and *Parenting Children for a Life of Confidence*).

111 Barbara Bassot, *The Reflective Practice Guide* (Routledge, 2016), p. 2.
112 Canavan et al., *Understanding Family Support*, p. 9.
113 Canavan et al., *Understanding Family Support*, p. 84.
114 Canavan et al., *Understanding Family Support*, p. 84.
115 Canavan et al., *Understanding Family Support*, p. 88.
116 Donald A. Schon, *Educating the Reflective Practitioner* (Jossey-Bass, 1987).
117 Schon, *Educating the Reflective Practitioner*, p. 26.
118 Barbara Bassot, *The Reflective Journal* (Palgrave Macmillan, 2013), p. 40.
119 Graham Gibbs, *Learning by Doing* (FEU, 1988).
120 Bassot, *The Reflective Practice Guide*, p. 105.
121 Eric Parsloe and Melville Leedham, *Coaching and Learning: Practical conversations to improve learning* (Kogan Page, 2009) p. 67.
122 Canavan et al., *Understanding Family Support*, p. 66.

Enabling all ages to grow in faith

Anna Chaplaincy
Barnabas in Schools
Holy Habits
Living Faith
Messy Church
Parenting for Faith

The Bible Reading Fellowship (BRF) is a Christian charity that resources individuals and churches and provides a professional education service to primary schools.

Our vision is to enable people of all ages to grow in faith and understanding of the Bible and to see more people equipped to exercise their gifts in leadership and ministry.

To find out more about our ministries and programmes, visit
brf.org.uk